Essential Malaysia

by

CHRISTINE OSBORNE

Christine Osborne is a travel writer with a
special interest in the East. She has travelled
widely in the Middle East, North Africa and
Southeast Asia. Among the books she has
written are *Essential Thailand, Essential Bali
and Jakarta* and *Essential Seychelles* in this
series. Christine is also a professional
photographer and took most of the
photographs in this book.

AA

Produced by AA Publishing

Written by Christine Osborne
Peace and Quiet section
by Paul Sterry
Series Adviser: Ingrid Morgan
Series Controller: Nia Williams
Copy Editor: Emma Stanford

Edited, designed and produced by
AA Publishing. Maps ©The
Automobile Association 1992.

Distributed in the United Kingdom
by the Publishing Division of The
Automobile Association, Fanum
House, Basingstoke, Hampshire,
RG21 2EA.

The contents of this publication are
believed correct at the time of
printing. Nevertheless, the
publishers cannot accept
responsibility for errors or
omissions, nor for changes in details
given. We have tried to ensure
accuracy in this guide, but things do
change and we would be grateful if
readers could advise us of any
inaccuracies they may encounter.

A CIP catalogue record for this book
is available from the British Library.

ISBN 0 7495 0311 4

Published by The Automobile
Association

Typesetting: Microset Graphics Ltd,
Basingstoke
Colour separation: BTB Colour
Reproduction, Whitchurch,
Hampshire
Printed in Italy by Printers SRL,
Trento

Front cover picture: Penang Wat
Chayamangkalaram

This book employs a
simple rating system to
help choose which
places to visit:

◆◆◆   do not miss

◆◆   see if you can

◆   worth seeing if
      you have time

INTRODUCTION

Malaysia's first major tourism campaign – 'Visit
Malaysia in 1990' – attracted over 15 million
visitors yet the country remains essentially
unspoilt and enticingly unexplored. Tourists
bound for Southeast Asia are finding a myriad
things to see and do in this lovely, unusual land.
Malaysia shares many similarities with its
neighbours in the region. As in Buddhist
Thailand the national religion, Islam in the case
of Malaysia, pervades every aspect of life. Like
Indonesia, Malaysia boasts spectacular scenery
from jungle-clad mountains to coral-girt islands.
Like Singapore (which seceded from the
federation in 1965) it offers superb duty-free
shopping. As well as a naturalist's paradise it is
a gourmet's delight – every town offers a choice
of local, Indian, Chinese and Nonya (or Straits
Chinese) cooking. The advantage Malaysia has
over its competitors is the combination of luxury
and adventure tourism on one ticket. You can
take a jacuzzi in the morning and shoot
white-water rapids in the afternoon. That night,

Sabak beach

dancing in a disco, you will wonder whether the day gone by was not a dream. Superb locations lie on capital Kuala Lumpur's doorstep. A half-day's drive takes you to Melaka (Malacca), redolent with powerful images of the past. Travel through Selangor to see why locals say that every road leads to a rubber-tree (or an oil-palm). In Sarawak you can eat an American breakfast in your hotel and dine with Dyaks in their traditional longhouse. Contrasts exist at every turn. Even a cab-ride to Chinatown is an adventure. Jungle treks, mountain-climbing, white-water rafting, scuba diving – all are organised by local tour operators. In luxurious hotels on the islands of Penang and Langkawi, waterskiing, paragliding and windsurfing are a stone's throw from your room. Most hotels have health clubs and tennis courts. Malaysia is one of the great golfing countries in the world and at current exchange rates, few places offer a better deal. Budget-travellers can live like tourists in Malaysia and tourists can live like kings. The country is also safe. Malay religious tolerance is such that although Islam is followed by two-thirds of the population and mosques are commonplace, there are even more Chinese temples and a strong Chinese community. A tangible Chinese influence is widely evident. Some places like the go-ahead island of Penang are wholly Chinese in character, while areas like the east coast are almost 100 per cent Malay.

This is where to go for a laid-back holiday. People walk slowly, wear little and contemplate a lot. No discos here. You will have to be happy with top-spinning and kite-flying. Your true *kampung,* or village, Malay seems like a flower-child of the sixties. The family unit remains strong. Occasions such as a wedding are looked forward to for months. An 'open house' policy extends to everyone – including tourists. Vibrant festivals are another bonus to a holiday in Malaysia. Occasions such as Chinese New Year, Hari Raya Puasa and Christmas are celebrated nationwide. There are also numerous harvest festivals especially enjoyed by ethnic tribes in Sabah and Sarawak. There is no 'right' time on the equator: Malaysia is hot, hot, hot. Just check it is not going to be hot and wet during the southwest monsoon or the southeast trade winds. And remember insect repellent. Even paradise can have mosquitoes.

Mount Kinabalu

Malay batik

BACKGROUND

The Land

Malaysia lies in the heartland of Southeast Asia, close to the equator. It consists of two quite separate regions. Peninsular Malaysia extends from the Straits of Johor, opposite Singapore, north to the Thai border. To the west, across the Straits of Malacca, lies the Indonesian island of Sumatra. To the east, 465 miles (750km) of the South China Sea separate Peninsular Malaysia (West Malaysia) and the eastern states of Sarawak and Sabah on the island of Borneo. The total area covers around 127,580 square miles (330,434sq km) and has a coastline extending nearly 3,000 miles (4,830km) from the Indian Ocean to the South China Sea.

Parallel ranges of mountains cross the peninsula from northwest to southeast, the highest in the centre. Low-lying alluvial plains, ideal for rice-growing, line the coasts. Much of Sabah and Sarawak is mountainous, culminating in mighty Gunung (Mount) Kinabalu in northern Sabah. Sarawak has extensive marshy coastal lowlands.

The hot, wet equatorial climate gives rise to exuberant plant growth. About 70 per cent of Malaysia is covered in dense rainforest with a huge diversity of plant and animal life. (See **Peace and Quiet**.)

History

The Niah cave paintings in Sarawak indicate that primitive man lived in Borneo as long as 40,000 years ago. Traces of early Orang Asli, or aboriginal tribes, have also been found in West Malaysia. Sanskrit and Chinese writings speak of the existence of the kingdom of Kedah about AD600–700. It is known that most of the states, or sultanates, probably came under the influence of the Indian Sri Vijayan Empire, established in Sumatra by AD900. The picture is clear by the 14th century, the start of what is known as the Golden Era of Malacca. Arab mariners spreading the message of Islam were among the first callers in square-rigged dhows. They were followed by Chinese merchants sailing bat-wing junks down the South China Sea to the fabled spice islands of Indonesia. The Malay peninsula was found to be a convenient

MALAYSIA

THAILAND

South   China

Kangar
Alor Setar
• Kota Bharu

■ Georgetown

Kuala Terengganu

PENINSULAR
MALAYSIA

■ Ipoh

• Kuantan

■ Kuala Lumpur
Shah Alam
• Seremban
• Melaka

Strait

of

Malacca

Johor Bahru
SINGAPORE

INDONESIA
(SUMATRA)

Guns on Selangor

half-way anchorage on the lucrative 'silks and
spices route' linking Asia, India and, ultimately,
Europe. Commerce centred on Malacca – by
the 15th century a Muslim kingdom – which
quickly grew into a prosperous port and a
powerful state. This aroused the interest of
European sea-powers and in 1511, it was taken
by the Portuguese. In a letter to Lisbon, a
Portuguese sailor describes Malacca's harbour
packed with foreign shipping and writes of the
babble of 84 different tongues in its waterfront
bazaar. *Bahasa Malaysia*, the national language
of Malaysia, is peppered with foreign words
from these early entrepreneurial exchanges.
In 1641, Malacca fell to the Dutch, who
eventually traded it with Britain in return for
Bencoolen in Sumatra in 1824. By the late 18th
century, British commercial interests in
Southeast Asia extended to Penang, which was
acquired for the East India Company from the
Sultan of Kedah by Captain Francis Light in
1786. This made three spheres of British
interest in Southeast Asia – Penang, Malacca
and Singapore, collectively known as the Straits

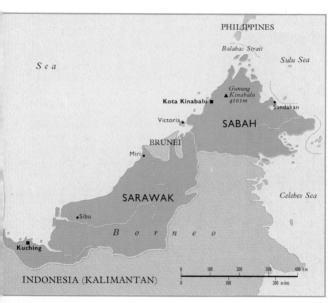

... and Kolah Lama

Settlements. British influence was also spreading to the island of Borneo, across the South China Sea. In 1840, an ex-Bengal guards officer – adventurer, James Brooke – was installed as the first white Rajah of Sarawak, a reward for helping the sultan crush a revolt. Founded in 1882, the British North Borneo Company began to acquire concessions. By 1888, Sarawak and North Borneo, now known as Sabah, had become British protectorates. All the states of the Malay peninsula, together with the Straits Settlements, had been brought under British rule by 1914. The conglomeration of states was known as Malaya.

World War II saw Malaya and the Borneo territories invaded by the Japanese in 1941, and the British were driven out. With encouragement and assistance from the Allies, Malay nationalists and Communist insurgents resisted the Japanese occupation for nearly four years. On Japan's surrender, in 1945, many nationalists sided with the Communists, and, united, they launched a campaign of anti-British terrorist violence which led to a State of

BACKGROUND

Malay dancer

Emergency being declared in 1948. Twelve years of hunt-and-destroy guerrilla warfare followed before the Emergency was finally lifted in 1960.

On 31 August 1957, Malaya was granted independence. Under the guidance of the Prime Minister of Malaya, the venerated Tunku Abdul Rahman, a federation of Malay states was formalised in 1963. The Federation of Malaysia comprises the 11 states in Peninsular, or West, Malaysia together with Sarawak and Sabah on the ex-British island of Borneo, known as East Malaysia. (Singapore seceded from the federation in 1965, but the two countries enjoy a close relationship.)

Society and Religion

The population of Malaysia in 1991 was some 18 million: a total of about 15 million living in Peninsular Malaysia, 1.7 million in Sarawak and 1.5 million in Sabah. There is a Malay majority of nearly nine million. A hard-working Chinese merchant class accounts for nearly five million with the balance made up of Indians, Eurasians and Indonesians. Increasing numbers of refugees from the southern Philippines are moving to Sabah.

The Orang Asli (native aboriginal) population of Peninsular Malaysia is estimated at 55,000. There are three main ethnic groups: Negrito, Senoi and Proto-Malay. The Negrito form around six tribal divisions and live mainly in the jungle-covered foothills of central Peninsular Malaysia. Gatherers and simple cultivators, they weave baskets and make cloth.

Senoi hill folk live from 4,000 feet (1,200m) upwards. They grow hill rice, tapioca, millet and bananas and supplement their diet by hunting and fishing. Their woven bamboo dwellings resemble the Iban or Dyak longhouses of Borneo. Proto-Malays form about 35 per cent of the Orang Asli population. They inhabit the upper riverine reaches of southern Peninsular Malaysia. The Temuan is the largest of the seven tribal groups. Another large tribe is the Jakun. These aborigines vary from jungle nomads wandering in search of food to simple farmers. There is more emphasis on the individual ownership of property than among

Bright city lights

other Orang Asli who follow the concept of communal ownership.

Of indigenous tribes in East Malaysia, the Iban, or Dyak, peoples make up 30 per cent of the population which numbers 25 different Orang Asli groups. Found throughout Sarawak, Ibans once depended on hunting and fishing. Today tourism has become profitable for communities of Iban living in their traditional longhouses. Others are increasingly attracted to the economic mainstream.

Sabah, too, has many aboriginal tribes, but intermarriage is common. The largest indigenous group are the Dusun, or Kadazans. Traditionally farmers, they practise slash-and-burn cultivation. The second group, the Bajau, are also involved in agriculture as well as buffalo- and pony-raising. Their expertise with horses is well known. The third group, the Murut, live in the lowlands and foothills of the hinterland. Some are still hunters and gatherers, while most practise farming, clearing an area and cultivating it before moving on.

The Malays who form the largest ethnic group are generally Muslims. There are also Muslims of Chinese, Indian and Pakistani ancestry. The most striking feature of Malaysia's multi-racial population is the tolerance of the various religions towards others – Christianity, Buddhism, Taoism and Hinduism as well as Sikhism, are practised alongside Islam. Some Orang Asli remain animists, but missionaries in East Malaysia have won many Christian converts. Testimony to Malaysia's religious freedom is the number of different places of worship – often just a few steps from each other.

National culture is based on ethnic Malay traditions with traits from other religions. Malay customs uphold Islamic values such as integrity, honesty, sincerity, brotherly care and respect, and especially belief in God. Islam is a true way of life and all orthodox Muslims in Malaysia adhere to Islamic teachings in their holy book, the Koran, and in the Hadiths, the sayings of the Prophet Muhammad. You will observe numerous Malaysian women – even tiny girls – wearing headscarfs in keeping with the strict precepts of Islamic fundamentalism.

BACKGROUND

Sailing weather

Economy and Government

While Malaysia was troubled by uncertainties affecting the world economy in the past, it now enjoys a balance of payments surplus. Looking at Kuala Lumpur and other major towns such as Penang and Kota Kinabalu, you can see signs of vigorous growth. High-rise office blocks and department stores are packed with locally manufactured goods.

Electrical goods, textiles, clothing and footwear, jewellery, optical and scientific goods, toys and sports equipment are all made in Malaysia. Crude petroleum has surpassed tin as the single largest export earner. Other major exports are palm oil, rubber, cocoa and timber. The East Malaysian state of Sabah contributes 35 per cent of total timber exports. Electrical goods, electronics, textiles and clothes are also important exports. Food, beverages and tobacco account for around five per cent of total manufactured goods. Processed rubber goods, surgical gloves and latex threads total nearly 20 per cent of world imports. Important customers for goods are the United States, Germany, Japan, Britain and fellow ASEAN (Association of Southeast Asian Nations) countries.

Malaysia has a parliamentary democracy based on free elections. The Head of State is His Majesty, the Yang Di-Pertuan Agong, a constitutional monarch who is elected by a conference of the state rulers for a five-year term. True power lies with the prime minister, who is the head of the government.

Visiting Malaysia

Fascinating Malaysia is made up of 13 states. There are 11 Malay states in Peninsular Malaysia, while the East Malay states of Sabah and Sarawak lie on the north coast of the large island of Borneo. Each state has characteristics of its own and offers an individual experience. Where you decide to go will depend on personal interests. The climate varies only a few degrees between north and south. It is hot everywhere and unless you choose the season carefully, it can be hot and wet. But from north to south, east to west, Malaysia has many charms and mysteries, traditions and cultures reflecting its exotic multi-racial population.

KUALA LUMPUR

The Federal capital Kuala Lumpur, or KL as it is known locally, is the dynamic gateway to Peninsular Malaysia. With more than a million inhabitants, the city has surged ahead since muddy beginnings at the junction of the rivers Kelang and Gombak which still flow through its centre. Meaning 'muddy estuary', KL was founded by tin prospectors in 1857. Today it is not only the federal capital, but the most developed city in Malaysia. One aspect, strikingly apparent to visitors, is the varied architecture. The Saracenic-style railway station, straight out of India, contrasts with a soaring highrise like the Dayabumi complex, while betwixt and between is a quaint assemblage of traditional Malay and colonial-style British. KL suffers serious traffic problems, but streets are clean and easy to navigate on foot with the help of a map. Everywhere are luxuriant patches of greenery left by city-planners – virgin jungle flourishes a few steps from the Shangri-La Hotel.

Mingling in KL are many nationalities whose cultures overlap but never clash – a rich mixture of Malays, Chinese, Indians, Arabs, Eurasians and Europeans. Most speak some English and treat tourists with courtesy. Theft is uncommon and beggars are conspicuously absent. The different races also contribute to the contrasting cuisines found in the capital, where four can dine for the price of one in a restaurant back home.

The clue to enjoying Kuala Lumpur is to take your time. Allow two or three days for shopping and sightseeing, or more if you are a golfer. The Royal Selangor Golf Club, considered to be one of the best in the world, is barely half a mile (1km) from the city centre. **Note:** Kuala Lumpur telephone numbers are prefixed by the code 03 (3 if dialling from abroad).

Sultan Abdul Samad Building, Kuala Lumpur

WHAT TO SEE

◆
BIRD PARK
A new, well-designed local family attraction near the Orchid Garden. Something less than the 5,000 birds advertised, but exotic species such as hornbills. Avoid at weekends. Shops, WC.
Open: daily 09.00–18.00 hrs.

◆◆
CENTRAL MARKET
Although rather contrived, this complex near Chinatown is worth a visit. Built in 1936 as a 'wet market', the building has been converted into a commercial and recreational centre with shops, food outlets, and exhibition centres. Malay cultural performances are staged daily on the rooftop, including displays of dance, martial arts and shadow plays.
Information: tel: 2746542.
Open: daily 10.00–22.00 hrs.

◆◆◆
CHINATOWN
Jalan Petaling is one of the busiest and most colourful parts of Kuala Lumpur and a great place to explore on foot. Open markets sell leather goods, clothing and textiles, junk jewellery and fake watches, fruit and herbs, cakes, cassettes and more. The Pasar Malam night market has good food-stalls. Watch your bag and valuables.

◆◆
LAKE GARDENS
This is one of Kuala Lumpur's natural landmarks. Popular with local families it offers picnic areas, boating on the lake, and refreshments stands selling snacks and drinks.

◆◆◆
MASJID JAME
A traditional Oriental/Islamic-style mosque at the confluence of the Kelang and Gombak rivers – the birthplace of KL. The pink and white façade, topped by a wealth of minarets and domes, recalls the Moghul mosques of northern India.
Open: 09.00–12.45 and 14.30–16.15 hrs except Friday.

◆◆
MASJID NEGARA (NATIONAL MOSQUE)
The 1960s national mosque is located near the railway station. The dome is cut in the shape of an 18-point star which represents the 13 Malaysian states and the five pillars of Islam. A further symbolic touch is provided by the 48 smaller domes similar to those on the Great Mosque in Mecca.
Open: Saturday to Thursday 09.00–18.00 and Friday 14.45–18.00 hrs. Visitors must be correctly dressed; women are required to wear a robe. Shoes must not be worn inside.

◆◆◆
MERDEKA SQUARE
Once the heart of colonial Kuala Lumpur, Merdeka Square is still a prime focus of the modern city. It is where the Union Jack was finally lowered on this corner of the British Empire at midnight on 31 August 1957, and replaced by the new flag of the Malaysian Federation. There are several important buildings around the central park, including the grandiose **Sultan Abdul Samad Building**, housing the Supreme Court, the **Selangor Club**, and **St Mary's Anglican Church**.

At prayer in the national mosque

◆◆ NATIONAL MONUMENT

This bronze sculpture, within the Lake Gardens, is dedicated to members of the Malay and Commonwealth forces who died during the Emergency. The monument is surrounded by a moat with cascading fountains and water lilies made of pewter.

◆◆◆ NATIONAL MUSEUM

On Jalan Travers, near the entrance to the Lake Gardens, the air-conditioned museum boasts excellent exhibitions of Malaysian history and culture, flora and fauna, and economic activities. Behind the imposing exterior, the Orang Asli and Nonya cultures are fully documented in fascinating displays. There is a complete Malay *kampung;* wondrous antique jewellery and fabrics; plus shadow puppets from around the world. Photography not allowed inside.
Open: daily 09.00–18.00 hrs; closed Fridays between 12.45–14.45 hrs. Admission free.

◆ PARLIAMENT HOUSE

Seat of the Senate and House of Representatives, the 18-storey parliament building can only be visited by appointment.

◆◆◆ RAILWAY STATION

Built in flamboyant Indo-Saracenic-style architecture between 1885 and 1911, this is a local landmark, festooned with turrets and minarets, arches and towers. The administrative headquarters, opposite, is of similar design. In the station, there are money-changers, restaurants, kiosks, a post office, WC facilities and the splendid old Station Hotel.

◆◆◆ SRI MARIAMMAN HINDU TEMPLE

The original building was founded in 1873. Within walking distance of the Central Market and Chinatown district, the temple is highly decorated with hundreds of colourful figures.

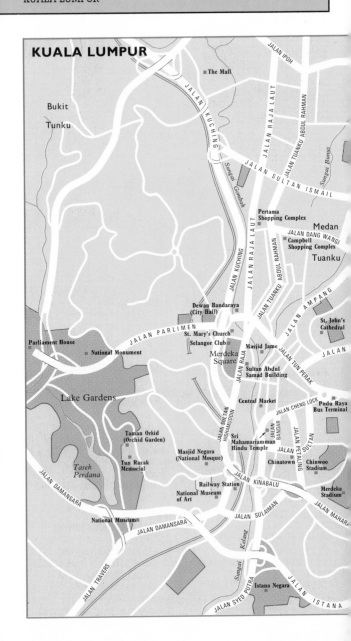

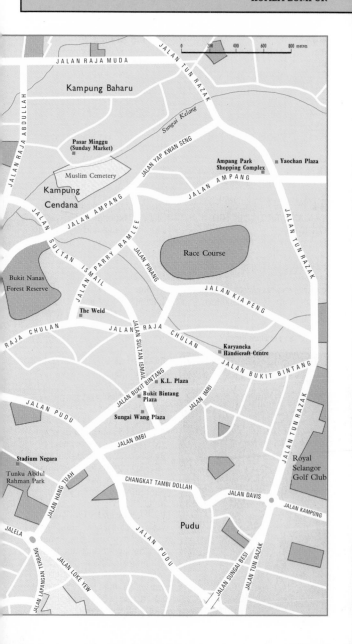

◆◆◆
SULTAN ABDUL SAMAD BUILDING

Incorporating Moorish arcades, gilded onion domes and a very British Colonial 136-foot (41m) high clock tower, this striking two-tone edifice was raised in the late 1890s to house the Colonial Government Secretariat. It stands on Jalan Raja, facing the Royal Selangor Club across Merdeka Square.

◆◆
TAMAN ORKID (ORCHID GARDEN)

Next to the Tun Abdul Razak Memorial (opposite Bird Park), these gardens display 3,000 dazzling varieties of exotic orchids together with local plants. *Open:* daily 10.00–16.00 hrs. Admission free.

Colourful souvenirs for sale

Getting Around

The best way to explore Kuala Lumpur is on foot, with the Tourist Development Corporation of Malaysia's (TDCM) *Kuala Lumpur Garden City of Lights Walking Map*, available free from tourist information centres. Otherwise, there are several alternative modes of transport:

By Bicycle: Explore Kuala Lumpur by mountain bike with an English-speaking guide. Sights include the Railway Station, National Mosque, the Lake Gardens and Parliament House. Duration 3 hours. *Enquiries:* Inter-Pacific, 75 Jalan Bukit Bintang, 55100 Kuala Lumpur (tel: 2480011).

By Bus: The bus station for Kuala Lumpur and Selangor is Klang Bus Station. Locker services are available here and in Pudu Raya, the bus station for all other places.

By Car: Self-drive is not advised although there are rental companies stationed at Subang Airport, hotels and shopping complexes. Avoid any form of sightseeing during the midday (11.00–14.30 hrs) and evening (16.00–18.00 hrs) rush-hours.

By Coach: Local travel agents offer numerous tours with hotel transfers/pick-ups included. Book direct or through your hotel.

By Trishaw and Taxi: Three-wheel trishaws can be hired in Chinatown, but agree on the fare before starting out. Taxis are metered. Fares remain among the cheapest in the world, but note that you have to add an extra 50 per cent to the meter after midnight.

Accommodation

Although Kuala Lumpur has a good selection of hotels, bookings are essential. Budget accommodation is listed in a free TDCM brochure available from tourist offices. It is worth noting that cheaper hotels are often noisy.

Coliseum Café and Hotel, 98–100 Jalan Tuanku Abdul Rahman (tel: 2926270). 10 rooms with fans, some with air-conditioning. Licensed bar and good restaurant with Western/Asian menu. Cheap.

Equatorial Hotel, Jalan Sultan Ismail (tel: 2617777). 300 air-conditioned rooms. All amenities. Near shopping centres. Moderate.

Federal Hotel, 35 Jalan Bukit Bintang (tel: 2489166). 450 air-conditioned rooms. Central for shopping. Moderate.

Fortuna Hotel, 87 Jalan Berangan (tel: 2419111). 98 rooms. Cheap.

Grand Central Hotel, 63 Jalan Putra (tel: 4410318). 142 rooms. Near the World Trade Centre. Cheap.

Hyatt Saujana, Subang International Airport Highway, Petaling Jaya (tel: 7461188). 230 rooms. Excellent hotel, minutes from airport. Quiet. Recommended. Expensive.

Kuala Lumpur Hilton, Jalan Sultan Ismail (tel: 2422222). 581 rooms, air-conditioning. First class amenities. Near Pudu Raya Bus Station and Central Market. Expensive.

Pudu Raya, 4th Floor, Pudu Raya Bus Station, Jalan Pudu (tel: 2321000). 200 rooms with excellent city views. Central location near Chinatown. Cheap.

Regent of Kuala Lumpur, 160 Jalan Bukit Bintang (tel: 2418000). 469 de luxe rooms. Excellent location near shopping complexes. Recommended. Expensive.

Shangri-La, 11 Jalan Sultan Ismail (tel: 2322388). 721 de luxe rooms in the heart of the business, shopping and entertainment district. Eight restaurants and bars. Shopping arcade with delicatessen. Business Centre. Recipient of many awards. Highly recommended. Expensive.

The Lodge, 2 Jalan Tengah (tel: 2420122). 50 rooms, air-conditioning. Good beds. Scruffy but pleasant. Small pool. Central location. Cheap.

YMCA, 95 Jalan Padang Belia (tel: 2741439). Some way out, but near a self-contained city-village with all requirements – cafés, films, markets. Basic accommodation for young travellers. Gym use. Membership not essential. Both sexes welcome.

Entertainment and Nightlife

While not in the same league as Bangkok or Jakarta, Kuala Lumpur offers a reasonable variety of after dark entertainment. Japanese karaoke lounges are very popular. Try **Club Fukiko**, 2nd Floor, Menara Promet, Jalan Sultan Ismail; **Karaoke Evergreen Lounge**, D7, Block D, Kuala Lumpur Plaza; **Lai Lai Karaoke Lounge**, G 11/15 Sungai Wang Plaza; **Ono Supper Club**, 2nd Floor, Wisma Selangor Dredging, Jalan Ampang; and **Tapagayo**, 2 Bintang Village, Jalan Bukit Bintang.

Discothèques
Current favourites include: **Club Oz**, Shangri-La Hotel, Jalan Tun Ismail; **Faces**, 103 Jalan Ampang; **Hearts**, Ampang Park Shopping Complex, Jalan Ampang; **Hippodrome Worldwide Discothèque**, Rooftop Ampang Park Shopping Complex, Jalan Ampang; **Limelight**, 3 Changkat Raja Chulan; **Phase II**, 370 Jalan Tun Razak; **Rumours**, Basement Hotel Merlin, Jalan Sultan Ismail; **Sapphire Discothèque**, Plaza Yow Chuan, Jalan Tun Razak; **Seventh Avenue**, 2nd Floor, Annexe Block Menara Apera ULG, Jalan Raja Chulan; **Stargazer**, Penthouse, Semua House, 6 Lorong Bunus; **Studio 30**, 30th Floor, Menara Promet, Jalan Tun Ismail; **The Turf**, 10 Jalan Kia Peng.

Cinemas
Cinemas open daily from as early as 11.00 hrs. The last programme usually begins at 21.15 hrs. Tickets are cheap, and most cinemas show English-language movies. Major tourist hotels have in-house video-movies.

Food and Drink
Kuala Lumpur rates high marks on the culinary front, and visitors are amazed by the remarkably modest prices. Eating places range from smart hotel restaurants and Chinese or seafood eateries to open-air market stalls. Several shopping centres have great value hawker centres. Reservations are advisable at all Kuala Lumpur restaurants on Fridays and weekends. Most establishments are full by 20.30 hrs.

A popular place is the **Yazmin** at 6 Jalan Kia Peng (tel: 2415655). Open for lunch and dinner, it serves a delicious buffet of spicy and non-spicy dishes, including vegetarian foods, and the cost of an evening meal includes a live cultural show. Other popular dining spots are: **Bunga Raya Restaurant**, Level 2, Putra World Trade Centre (tel: 4422999); **Sate Ria**, 9 Jalan Tuanku Abdul Rahman (tel: 2927860), and several other locations; **Rasa Utara**, Bukit Bintang Plaza (tel: 2488363); and **Nelayan Floating Restaurant**, Titiwangsa Lake Gardens (tel: 4228400). There are hundreds of superb Chinese restaurants in Kuala Lumpur of which the following are recommended: **Shang Palace**, at the Shangri-La Hotel (tel: 2322388); **Village Restoran**, 320 Jalan Tun Razak (tel: 2418750); **Regent Court Chinese Restaurant**, Jalan Sultan Ismail (tel: 2422232); **Restoran Teochew**, 272 Jalan Changkat

Thambi Dollah (tel: 2416572); and **Mak Yee Restaurant**, Level 3, 32 Jalan Sultan Ismail (tel: 2482404). **Dreamland Drink and Food Garden**, 14 Jalan Tun Perak (behind the Equatorial Hotel) is a consistently popular Chinese/ seafood restaurant (tel: 2482391). Other suggested restaurants: **Castell Grill**, 81 Jalan Bukit Bintang (tel: 2428328); **Decanter Restaurant**, 7 Jalan Setiakasih 5 (tel: 2552507); **Kenanga Lounge**, Medan Mara, Jalan Raja Laut (tel: 2933790); **L'Espresso**, G22, 23, 24 Wisma Stephens, Jalan Raja Chulan (tel: 2414699); **Le Coq D'or**, 121 Jalan Ampang (tel: 2429732); **The Hop Sack**, 1st Floor, KL Plaza (tel: 2437429); **Yuyi Grill and Lounge**, Loke Yew Building, Jalan Belanda (tel: 2984698); and **Memory Lane**, 1st Floor, Annexe Block, Menara Apera ULG, Jalan Raja Chulan (tel: 2415118).
Kuala Lumpur also has Western fast-food branches of Kentucky Fried Chicken, McDonald's and Dunkin' Doughnuts.

Shopping
Kuala Lumpur is a shopper's paradise. At the top end of the market there are boutiques selling clothes by Christian Dior, Gucci, Mondi and popular Levi Strauss jeans. Watches, cameras and locally-made electronic goods are bargain priced. Sports equipment costs a third of its price in Europe. There are excellent buys in beautifully tooled leather belts and bags. Top-selling cassettes cost the price of a packet of king size cigarettes in England. And you will find a dazzling array of handicrafts – pewter, batik, silverware – from all over Malaysia. Hunt around and compare prices. Market traders expect to bargain but prices are fixed in department stores. Major credit cards are widely accepted. Clothing shops make alterations while you wait. Tailor-made suits or dresses take about 48 hours.

Shopping in the Central Market

Shopping Complexes

Ampang Park, Jalan Ampang, is crammed with bargains. **Bukit Bintang Plaza**, Jalan Bukit Bintang, is conveniently located in one of the best shopping areas. The **Campbell Shopping Complex**, Jalan Dang Wangi, offers a huge variety of cheap locally made goods. As does **City Square**, Jalan Tun Razak. Don't miss the multi-storey **Dayabumi Complex** on Jalan Sultan Hishamuddin, not far from Merdeka Square; and the **KL Plaza**, Jalan Bukit Bintang, is good, cheap and centrally located. **Lot 10**, Jalan Sultan Ismail, is one of the most de luxe shopping complexes in Asia. Its exclusivity is reflected in the prices. On the other hand, **Pertama Shopping Complex**, Jalan Dang Wangi, provides great value economy shopping for most requirements. **Sungai Wang Plaza**, Jalan Sultan Ismail, located near several tourist hotels, is joined to Metro Jaya and Bukit Bintang Plaza. A dedicated shopper could spend days here. **The Mall**, Jalan Putra (opposite the Pan Pacific Hotel), is very popular with tourists. The top and ground floors are economy restaurants and there is everything you need under one roof. **The Weld**, Jalan Raja Chulan, offers a good choice of locally made clothing at moderate prices. **Yaochan Plaza**, Jalan Ampang, is a smart, multi-storey complex with moderate prices.

Malaysian Handicraft Outlets

Batek Malaysia Berhad, Wisma Kraftangan, Jalan Tun Perak (and 114 Jalan Bukit Bintang), sells batik and handicrafts, as well as hosting exhibitions. **Central Market** offers plenty of variety, and daily cultural performances. The handicrafts exhibitions at **Infokraf Malaysia** in the Dayabumi Complex, Jalan Sultan Hishamuddin, are a must; and the **Karyaneka Handicraft Village**, Jalan Raja Chulan, offers craft sales and exhibitions (*open:* 09.30–17.30 hrs). There are further branches at the National Museum and Subang International Airport. **10 Kia Peng** is a great arts centre with a gallery, craft stables and a hawker centre (11.00–22.00 hrs). Contemporary works by local artists are displayed at **Kumpulan Anak Alam Gallery** in Central Market. The **Selangor Pewter Factory** has several showrooms in KL; check out the central one at 231 Jalan Tuanku Abdul Rahman.

Shopping Areas

Several areas in Kuala Lumpur have a concentration of shops which makes for both diversity and value:

Jalan Tuanku Abdul Rahman/ Jalan Chow Kit
Jalan Petaling/Jalan Sultan/Jalan Bandar
Jalan Bukit Bintang/Jalan Sultan Ismail
Jalan Masjid India/Jalan Melayu/ Lorong Bunus
Saturday Pasar Malam: this Night Market is organised every Saturday night on a sealed-off stretch of Jalan Tuanku Abdul Rahman. Among wares on sale are clothes, batik cloth, handicrafts, household items and a delicious variety of foodstuffs and sweetmeats.

PENINSULAR MALAYSIA

STATE OF JOHOR

The State of Johor encloses the
southern tip of Peninsular
Malaysia, the only state with
both east and west coastlines.
The capital, Johor Bahru, is
linked by a causeway to
Singapore. Most tourist visitors
are in transit, but more people
are stopping off to enjoy the
superb tropical islands off
Mersing on the east coast. Johor
is a major producer of pepper
and pineapples. The father of
modern Johor is Sultan Abu
Bakar, who transferred the
capital from Telok Belanga in
Singapore to Johor Bahru in
1866. The state population
exceeds two million.

JOHOR BAHRU

A busy, noisy town, Johor Bahru
caters to a constant stream of
travellers, businessmen, local
holidaymakers and tourists. The
road journey to Kuala Lumpur is
a nightmare – wise travellers
take the train. There is a day
and a night service in both
directions. A half-day city tour

*Traditional remedies are still
available from Chinese herbalists*

will cover all the important
sights, including a stop at Vista
Point for a panoramic view of
the Straits of Johor.

WHAT TO SEE

◆◆
CAUSEWAY

Peninsular Malaysia and the
island of Singapore have been
linked by a causeway since
1924. A road, rail and
pedestrian artery, the Causeway
is 3,464 feet (1,056m) long, its
foundations descend to a depth
of 75 feet (23m) below sea-level,
and there are immigration and
customs posts located at each
end.

◆
ISTANA BESAR

Built in 1866, the former royal
palace contains historic records,
objets d'art and crown jewels
belonging to the royal family of
Johor. There are extensive
gardens, refreshments and WC
facilities, and a souvenir shop.
Open: daily 09.00–12.00 hrs
except Fridays.

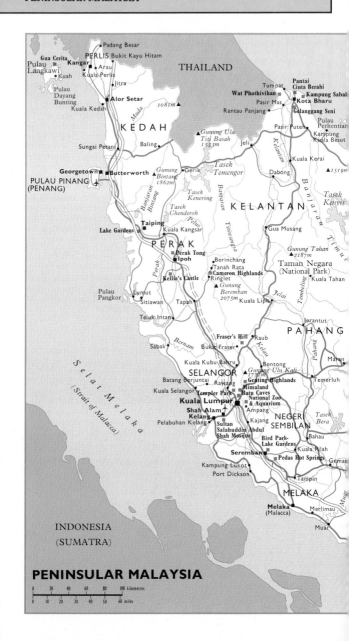

PENINSULAR MALAYSIA

◆
ISTANA BUKIT SERENE
Founded in 1933, this is the current residence of the Sultan of Johor. External view only.

◆◆
SULTAN ABU BAKAR MOSQUE
A fine Moorish-style mosque built in 1900, and located near the Istana Besar. Visitors must be properly attired.

Accommodation
It is advisable to reserve accommodation in advance for the weekend.
Holiday Inn, Jalan Dato Sulaiman, Century Garden (tel: (07) 323800). 200 rooms with air-conditioning, TV, international direct dialling. Moderate.
Merlin Inn, 10 Jalan Bukit Meldrum (tel: (07) 237400). 104 rooms on the seafront, five minutes from the Causeway. Business centre. Moderate.
Rasa Sayang Bharu Hotel, 10 Jalan Dato Dalam (tel: (07) 248600). 100 rooms. Cheap.
Straits View Hotel, 1-D Jalan Skudai (tel: (07) 241402). Popular hotel with 30 rooms. Cheap.

Food and Drink
Johor abounds in cheap eating places. The cuisine is mainly Chinese, and local seafood is excellent.

Shopping
The Holiday Plaza in Jalan Sulaiman is a large, modern shopping and food-stall complex. Malay handicrafts are on sale at **Syarikat Sri Mawar**. Some outlets sell Aw pottery. Avoid shopping at weekends when Johor is thronged with Singaporeans taking advantage of the exchange rate.

WHAT TO SEE IN JOHOR

◆◆ AYER HITAM

54 miles (87km) from Johor Bahru

Ayer Hitam is known as the 'town that never sleeps' because everyone using the north–south highway stops here to eat and take a break. Near Kampung Macap is the renowned **Aw Pottery factory**. The original Aw pottery was started over one hundred years ago by a ceramics artist from China. More than 100 craftsmen make every item by hand, using the same kickwheel used by potters in China over a thousand years ago. Aw pottery has a distinctive design and glaze. Visitors are welcome to look around the showroom, and can order custom-made pottery to their own designs.

◆◆ DESARU

70 miles (112km) from Johor Bahru

An integrated tourist complex situated on the unspoilt east coast, this is a very popular local resort where Japanese are a familiar sight on the golf course. Other activities include swimming, sailing, windsurfing and trekking in the virgin bush.

Accommodation

Desaru View Hotel, PO Box 71, 81907 Kota Tinggi (tel: (07) 821221). 134 rooms. International standard. Expensive.
Desaru Golf Hotel, Tanjung Penawar, PO Box 50, 81907 Kota Tinggi (tel: (07) 821101). 100 rooms with first class facilities. Moderate to expensive.

Food and Drink

Western/Malay/Chinese menus are available in the tourist hotels. Local food-stalls at weekends.

◆ JOHOR LAMA (OLD JOHOR)

18 miles (30km) from Johor Bahru

This small village on the Johor river was the Sultanate's capital during the 16th century. Also the scene of various archaeological discoveries and a restored fort.

◆◆ KOTA TINGGI

35 miles (56km) from Johor Bahru

Kota Tinggi is famous for its cascades which lie nine miles (15km) northeast of the town. The main waterfall is 105 feet (32m) high, and icy water splashes down into a pool below. Take a picnic, but avoid the weekends. There are changing rooms, refreshments and food-stalls available.

Glossy star-fruit is just one local speciality you can try here

◆
MERSING
85 miles (138km) from Johor Bahru

On the east coast of Johor, this small fishing port is the departure point for Tioman Island. The **Mersing Rest House** is pleasant for an overnight stop if catching the morning boat. Cheap. (See **Pulau Tioman**.)

◆◆
PULAU RAWA
90-minute boat ride from Mersing (above)

A small, but developed holiday island off the east coast. Chalets built on stilts offer basic accommodation a few yards/ metres from the beach. Marine sports include swimming, fishing, snorkelling and scuba-diving. Crowded at weekends. For bookings contact **Rawa Safaris**, The Tourist Centre, Jalan Abu Bakar, Mersing (tel: (07) 791204/5).

◆◆◆
PULAU TIOMAN
3 hrs by boat/1 hr by hydrofoil from Mersing (above)

Beautiful Pulau Tioman is rated by island-hoppers. Jungle-clad hills rise behind white sand beaches with a handful of quaint fishing villages dotted around the coast. There is a chance to sample the luxuriant jungle interior by taking the footpath across the island from Kampung Tekek (Lizard Village) on the west coast to Kampung Juara (Catfish Village) on the east. The walk should take around three-and-a-half hours.

Other activities include tennis, golf, fishing and diving. All major hotels have a watersports centre where diving and other gear may be hired.

Diving trips can be arranged in advance through **Ben's Diving Centre**, Salang Beach, Pulau Tioman. Stock up on toiletries and other personal requirements before leaving the mainland. Western and Chinese cuisine, plus an abundance of seafood is available in the hotels. The **Sri Nelayan** restaurant in Tioman Island Resort is recommended.

Accommodation
Island hotels range from simple beachside accommodation to sophisticated resorts, and prices range accordingly.

ABC Huts, Tioman Island. 20 huts, ideal for budget-travellers. Rock bottom prices.

Samudra Swiss Cottage, Tioman Island (tel: (07) 248728). 20 rooms. Cheap.

Tioman Island Resort, PO Box 4, 86807 Mersing (tel: (09) 445445). 185 up-market rooms. Popular with Western tourists. Moderate to expensive.

How to Get to Tioman:
Tioman is accessible by passenger boat (3 hrs) and hydrofoil (1 hr) from Mersing. Landings are subject to tides. Quick Silver Ferry operates a boat service from Singapore to Tioman.

By air there are daily flights from Kuala Lumpur (flight time one hour). Special two-to-three day package tours of Tioman include transport and accommodation. The Johor Bahru-Mersing Express bus operates a scheduled service on Sundays. Book seats well in advance.

STATE OF KEDAH

One of the small northwestern coastal states on Peninsular Malaysia, Kedah covers a region of 3,639 square miles (9,425sq km). The state capital is Alor Setar. The major crop is rice, fishing is important, and tourism is being developed on the Langkawi Islands.

ALOR SETAR

This busy commercial centre (60 miles/96km north of Butterworth) is of little interest unless travelling en route to Thailand or the Langkawi Islands. The **Merlin Inn Kedah** is a moderately priced hotel for a night stop. There are plenty of cheap eating-places, and a Wednesday market.

WHAT TO SEE

◆
BELAI BESAR
opposite the Zahir Mosque
Built in 1898, this wooden building, which combines Thai and Malay architectural styles, is where the Sultan gives audiences to the people on his birthday and festive occasions.

◆
BELAI NOBAT
near the Belai Besar
The repository of the royal orchestra houses the instruments of the royal musicians – three drums, a gong and a flute. These are played only on ceremonial occasions by an exclusive band of hereditary musicians. A visit to the *nobat* is a must during the installation of the Yang Di-Pertuan Agong, or Paramount Ruler of Malaysia.

◆
MUZIUM NEGERI (STATE MUSEUM)
on the airport road
Designed in a combination of Thai and Malay architectural styles, the museum houses interesting exhibits illustrating the cultural heritage of the State of Kedah. Admission free.

WHAT TO SEE IN KEDAH

◆◆
KUALA KEDAH
7 miles (12km) from Alor Setar
A busy fishing village with excellent seafood dining at the mouth of the Kedah river.

◆◆
PANTAI MERDEKA
37 miles (60km) from Alor Setar
A long sandy beach lined with coconut palms. Good swimming ensures crowds of local families at weekends and holidays.

◆◆◆
PULAU LANGKAWI
ferries take 45 mins from Kuala Perlis; 1 hr from Kuala Kedah
Jewel in the crown of Kedah's tourist attractions, this group of almost 100 islands lies 19 miles (30km) off Peninsular Malaysia in the Indian Ocean. Some islands have been turned into luxurious tourist resorts with superb hotels. Others remain rustic. The largest island, Langkawi, counts around 40,000 people. The majority live in **Kuah**, the main town, which is well supplied with good seafood restaurants, and souvenir and duty-free shopping opportunities.
There are several pleasant excursions to be made from

Kuah, all within an easy 18-mile (30km) radius of the town. The unusual limestone rock formations of **Gua Cerita** (the Cave of Legends) have been painted with writings from the Koran. Outdoor attractions include the **Telaga Tujah** (seven pools), a popular picnic spot where a series of cascades tumble into pools; and **Telaga Air Panas** (hot water pools) fed by natural hot springs. There is a two-hour boat trip from Pantai Cenang to **Pulau Dayang Bunting** (Island of the Pregnant Maiden), a sizeable island with a legendary magic lake. Drinking the lake's waters is supposed to help barren women to conceive. Take a picnic and charter a boat for the day. Pulau Langkawi's beaches are renowned. Some of the best are the black sands of **Pantai Pasir Hitam** (12 miles/19km from Kuah); **Pantai Teluk Burau**, a long west coast beach near the airport; **Pantai Cenang** on the southern peninsula; **Pantai Tengah** at the southern tip of Langkawi; and **Pantai Datai**, a palm-lined north coast beach facing Pulau Anak Dantai island. **Pantai Rhu** (14 miles/22km from Kuah) is good for diving. At low tide, there is a sandbar across to an island. Take a picnic, but check tide times.

Accommodation

Burau Bay Resort, Teluk Burau (tel: (04) 911061). Luxury resort spread along the sandy white beach lining Burau Bay. 150 rooms with air-conditioning, tea/coffee making facilities, TV, international direct dialling, mini-bar. Tennis courts and watersports including scuba, windsurfing, water-skiing, paragliding. Bicycles and jeeps for rental. Baby-sitters are available. Highly recommended for family holidays. Expensive.
Mutiara Beach Resort, Tanjung Rhu (tel: (04) 788488). 68 rooms. Cheap.
Pelangi Beach Resort, Pantai Cenang (tel: (04) 789789). De luxe hotel with 300 rooms, all with air-conditioning, international direct dialling, TV, mini-bar, tea/coffee making facilities. Handicapped persons' rooms and wheelchairs for disabled visitors. Expensive.
Semarak Langkawi, Pantai Cenang (tel: (04) 789777). 32 air-conditioned chalets near beach and airport. Moderate.

Food and Drink

Langkawi is renowned for superb fresh seafood. There are plenty of cheap Malay, Chinese and Indian eating places in Kuah. For a special night out, try **The Spice Market Restaurant** (tel: 789789) at the Pelangi Beach Resort. It serves both international and local cuisine; as does the **Burau Terrace-Restaurant** (tel: 911061).

How to Get to Langkawi:

MAS operates direct daily flights to the island from Kuala Lumpur and Penang. The ferry from Kuala Kedah takes an hour. There is a shorter 45-minute ferry crossing from Kuala Perlis. A once-monthly ferry service links Langkawi with Penang, departing Penang on Friday and returning on Sunday. Cheap and cheerful – one for the budget-traveller.

STATE OF KELANTAN

The State of Kelantan occupies the isolated northeast corner of Peninsular Malaysia, where recorded history begins around 3000BC. Kelantan is acknowledged to be the cradle of Malay culture, and it is the home of traditional pastimes such as shadow plays *(wayang kulit)*, kite-flying and top-spinning, most in evidence during festivals. The coast is quiet – no de luxe developments here, just a rustic lifestyle which attracts visiting backpackers. The state economy is based on rubber, palm oil and rice. Fishing is the main activity in coastal *kampungs*; women are employed in small cottage industries. Kelantan is renowned for its delicate handicrafts such as silverware, songket weaving and bamboo-work. With a population more than 95 per cent Malay, this is

one of the three states with an Islamic-style state government. Visitors should dress with consideration for local values. The state capital, Kota Bharu, is linked by daily flights with Kuala Lumpur and Penang, and Express Bus service to Kuala Teregannu.

KOTA BHARU

The state capital is a pleasant town on the banks of the Kelantan river. Most of the historic landmarks are located near Merdeka Square, and are easily visited on foot. The Court House and Tourist Information Centre are both housed in fine old buildings. There is a busy open-air eating spot near the bus station on Jalan Hamzak, and the Pasar Malam (night market) is highly rated for a delicious, cheap evening meal (see **Food and Drink**).

Freshly cooked at the night market

Batik, made locally in Kelantan

WHAT TO SEE

◆◆◆
CENTRAL MARKET
near the SKMK Town Bus Station
Kota Bharu's covered market is one of the most colourful in all Malaysia. Women vendors sit in the centre surrounded by a profusion of exotic fruits and vegetables bathed in light from the glass roof. They have a distinct dislike of photographers, but there is a great view from the upstairs balcony. Stalls on the first floor sell dried foods, spices and cakes, plus there are food stalls serving local specialities such as *nasi campur*. On the second floor, check out the variety of batik cloth and handicrafts. The market is open daily. Allow at least an hour to see it.

◆◆◆
GELANGGANG SENI (CULTURAL CENTRE)
on Jalan Mahmud
Displays of top-spinning, kite-flying, shadow plays, *silat* (a form of self defence) and drum playing are normally held on Mondays, Wednesdays and Saturdays from February to October. Check with the Tourist Office for details.

◆◆◆
MERDEKA SQUARE
Erected as a war memorial after 1945, the square is surrounded by the town's most important buildings: the 1922 State Mosque; the old Istana Balai Besar (royal palace), still enclosed by the original fortress walls and featuring fine local woodcarving; and the elegant 100-year-old Istana Jahar. The latter has been converted into the State Museum furnished

with an interesting range of exhibits illustrating local crafts, history and culture.

Accommodation

Satisfactory tourist hotels are in short supply, but here are some suggestions:

Perdana Hotel, PO Box 222, Jalan Mahmud (tel: (09) 785000). 136 rooms in the town centre. Moderate.

Perdana Resort, Jalan Kuala Pak Amat, Box 121, Pantai Cinta Berahi (tel: (09) 785222). 50 chalets in pastel hues set back from the beach just north of the town. TV, international direct dialling. Mediocre food and service. Popular with local families. Moderate.

Hotel Indah, 236-B Jalan Tengku Besar (tel: (09) 785081). 44 air-conditioned rooms in good location. Basic facilities; Chinese and seafood restaurant. Cheap.

HB Village, Pantai Cinta Berahi, Lot 66 and 67 Mukim Badang (tel: (09) 747470). Longhouse-style chalets near the beach, some with air-conditioning. Popular with local families; quieter during the week. Cheap rates include breakfast.

Food and Drink

The Pasar Malam (night market) sells delicious snacks and meals. Walk around and watch the cooks at work. Tasty local dishes include *ayam Percik*, reckoned the best in the country. This is barbecued chicken on a skewer served with a thick coconut sauce. Western fare is served at the **Perdana Hotel** and the **Rebana Coffee-House**. The **Golden Jade Seafood Restaurant** has a good Cantonese menu.

Shopping

Kelantan is famous for gold and silverware, batik and songket cloth, pottery, bamboo-ware, wood carvings, shadow puppets *(wayang kulit)* and kites among other things. Many simple crafts are sold on the street and in market-places. **Syarikat Kraftangan** on Jalan Sultan (near Merdeka Square) is a one-stop centre for souvenirs; and the second floor of Central Market is the place to look for batik and many other handicrafts. The shops along Jalan Temenggong have plenty to offer; or watch the silversmiths at work on Jalan Sultanah Zainab. On the road to Pantai Cinta Berahi small cottage factories produce batik and songket. For local black pottery, head south to the village of Mambong. If time is short, **Bazaar Buluh Kubu** on Jalan Hulu Kota, in the heart of Kota Bharu, sells local goods as well as items from Thailand and Indonesia. Duty-free shopping is available at Rantau Panjang and Kayu Hitam.

WHAT TO SEE IN KELANTAN

◆◆

MASJID KAMPUNG LAUT

6 miles (10km) south of Kota Bharu

Reputed to be the oldest mosque in Malaysia, the 18th-century Masjid Kampung Laut is built entirely of wood without the use of a single nail. Moved from its original site, on the banks of the Kelantan river because of flood danger, the splendid old building now has to put up with a rather dreary site beside a busy road.

◆ PANTAI CINTA BERAHI
6 miles (10km) north of Kota Bharu

To reach the famous 'Beach of Passionate Love', take Jalan Pejabat Pos Lama, then follow Route DI from Old Chinatown. The swimming here is good, but the beach is a bit disappointing, and none too clean. However, it is a pleasant drive winding through a series of picturesque small villages selling cottage crafts. Look out for songket weaving at Kampung Penambang (2 miles/3km).

◆◆ PANTAI DASAR SABAK
8 miles (13km) from Kota Bharu

It is hard to believe this pleasant, palm tree-lined beach was the scene of the Japanese landings in 1941. Kampung Sabak is a traditional fishing village less than a mile further down the coast. Be there when colourful *bangau* (fishing boats) return around 15.00 hrs. As each boat reaches the beach, it is pulled up by relatives and friends. If you want to see real bargaining, watch the carry-on between wholesalers, usually Malay women, and the boat-owners.

◆◆ RANTAU PANJANG
24 miles (39km) southwest of Kota Bharu

Shoppers and souvenir hunters often make a trip to this border town famous for its bargains. Golok, on the Thai side, is a free-wheeling bazaar of a town with cheap buys in clothes and fake watches.

◆ WAT PHOTHIVIHAN
9 miles (15km) north of Kota Bharu

Pride of place in the small Malay-Thai village of Kampung Jambu goes to the 130-foot (40m) long reclining Buddha – another contender in the heavyweight contest to build the largest Buddha in Southeast Asia.

Fishermen and their families land their boats with the day's catch on to the beach at Sabak

STATE OF MELAKA (MALACCA)

Melaka, or Malacca, on the west coast of Peninsular Malaysia, is the best known Malay state. Its overseas contacts go back to the heady days of entrepreneurial activity in the 16th and 17th centuries. The state capital, Melaka, was one of the most prosperous ports in Asia. Silks, spices, ceramics, ivory, opium, tobacco and countless other goods were traded in its waterfront bazaar. In 1511, Melaka was captured by the Portuguese who built palaces and churches and raised fortifications around the town. They were succeeded by the Dutch in 1641, who introduced Flemish-style architecture. It is this rich repository of European buildings alongside ancient temples and mosques that makes Melaka so interesting. Facing across the Selat Melaka (Strait of Malacca), about 90 miles (145km) from Kuala Lumpur, it is easily accessible on good roads. The Jebat Express Bus Service from Kuala Lumpur is fast and cheap (tel: (06) 222503 for details).

The waterfront at Melaka

MELAKA

Melaka is an engaging old town steeped in history. The Portuguese, Dutch and British have all left their architectural calling cards. On a walk through the old shop-houses along the canal, you will see architectural gems down every narrow street, and fine antiques are discovered in the most unlikely places. Local temples and mosques are among the oldest in Peninsular Malaysia. You are also likely to taste some of the best food in Malaysia. Melaka is renowned for the subtle, yet exquisite tastes of Peranakan or Nonya (Straits Chinese) cooking. A pleasant way of sightseeing is a cruise up the Malacca river. Boats leave the small jetty near the Tourist Office. (Enquiries, tel: 236538.) Look out for the old Chinese clan buildings and unique Malaccan-style wooden houses with tiled stone steps and long verandahs. Allow two days to discover Melaka. A guided city tour is recommended, or rent a shared taxi with an English-speaking driver. Trishaws are expensive, so why not try a bullock-cart ride around Padang Pahlawan? Malacca is the only state in Malaysia which offers this novel form of transport.

WHAT TO SEE

◆◆◆
BABA NONYA HERITAGE MUSEUM

50 Jalan Tun Tan Cheng Lock
This privately-owned museum offers a unique insight into the heritage of the Straits Chinese (Nonyas) in Malaysia. Displayed in three adjoining houses, a curious mix of neo-classic English and Dutch with a handful of Greco-Roman columns for good measure, the richly furnished interiors illustrate the opulent lifestyle of the Nonyas at the turn of the century. The magnificent teak staircase is a carved wood masterpiece, huge embroideries cover the walls and furniture glitters with inlaid mother-of-pearl. Some rooms display early Dutch and English furniture. Guides are family members. *Open:* daily 10.00–15.30 hrs. Admission charge.

◆◆
BUKIT CHINA

In 1459, the famous maritime adventurer and envoy of the Ming emperor, Admiral Cheng Ho, sent his daughter to marry the Sultan of Malacca. Her entourage consisted of 500 ladies-in-waiting and to accommodate them, the Sultan gave them Chinese Hill (Bukit China) as a residence. The hill, in east Melaka, now supports the largest Chinese cemetery outside China with more than 12,000 graves, many of which date from Ming times.

◆◆◆
CHENG HOON TENG TEMPLE
on Jalan Tokong

Dating from 1646, this is reputed to be the oldest Chinese temple in Malaysia. The eaves are decorated with mythological figures made from chip-porcelain, and the lacquerwork of the interior is outstanding. The temple's main altar is dedicated to the Goddess of Mercy – guardian of fishermen – and the railings above depict the life story of Buddha. All the materials used in the construction were imported from China.

◆◆
CHRIST CHURCH
at the foot of St Paul's Hill

A fine example of pure Dutch 18th-century architecture with materials, in this case, shipped all the way from Holland. Each of the church's massive roof beams was carved from a single tree. Note the plaque at the entrance and the painting of *The Last Supper* near the pulpit.

◆◆◆
GEREJA ST PAUL (ST PAUL'S CHURCH)
on St Paul's Hill

The picturesque ruins of 'St Paul's Church overlook Melaka and the Straits. Founded by the Portuguese in 1521, the church was called Duarte Coelho, until the Dutch renamed it and turned it into an extension of the fort, complete with gun embrasures still visible today. Inside the main structure is a pit which once held the body of St Francis Xavier, later enshrined in the Bom Jesus Cathedral in Goa, India. It is a stiff climb directly up St Paul's Hill. By far the easiest way is to walk anti-clockwise around the hill to the rear stairs, by the Porta de Santiago. These bring you to the entrance to St Paul's.

◆◆
MASJID KAMPUNG HULU (KAMPUNG HULU MOSQUE)
on Jalan Kampung Hulu

This, the oldest mosque in Malaysia, dates from 1728. Its unusual architectural style is unique to Malacca.

◆◆
MASJID TRANQUERAH (TRANQUERAH MOSQUE)
Jalan Tranquerah

This lovely mosque lies on the road to Port Dickson. Its architectural style is of a type only found in Malacca: instead of minarets, a pagoda-type structure is used for making the prayer-call. Within the grounds is the tomb of the Sultan of Johor who signed the cession of Singapore to Sir Stamford Raffles in 1819.

The Portuguese, Dutch and British have all left their mark on Melaka

◆◆
MEMORIAL HALL
off Jalan Parameswara
Built in 1912, the Memorial Hall once housed the British Colonial Malacca Club. Today it displays artefacts, film and documentation illustrating the lead-up to Malaya's independence.

◆
PADANG PAHLAWAN
Padang Pahlawan, the 'Warrior's Field', was the setting for Prime Minister Tunku Abdul Rahman's proclamation of independence on 20 February 1956.

◆◆
PERKAMPUNGANG PORTUGIS (PORTUGUESE SQUARE)
Jalan D'Albuquerque (1¾ miles/ 3km from town centre)
Melaka still has a small Portuguese community of around one thousand, and most live in the Portuguese Settlement near the beach. They speak the ancient Portuguese dialect *Cristão* among themselves, are devout Catholics and still regard Portugal as their homeland. On Saturday evenings there is a cultural show featuring Portuguese music, singing and dancing. Local shops sell authentic Portuguese foods and crafts.

◆◆
PORTA DE SANTIAGO
off Jalan Kota

The Santiago Gateway is the last vestige of a great fort built by the Portuguese in 1511. The fortress, which once enclosed St Paul's Hill, was badly damaged during the Dutch siege, restored in 1670, and finally all but razed by the British during the 19th century. Only the timely arrival of Sir Stamford Raffles saved the gate for posterity. Open access.

◆
ST JOHN'S FORT
1¾ miles (3km) from the town centre

Built on St John's Hill, close to Bukit China, the fort was originally a Portuguese chapel, later fortified by the Dutch. It guarded the seafront and still affords a fine view of the Straits and Melaka.

◆◆◆
STADTHUYS
bottom of St Paul's Hill

Built in the 1650s, the Dutch-style Town Hall faces the clock tower on Red Square, so named for the lashings of paint coating the surrounding buildings. It once housed the Dutch governor of Malacca and his staff, safely ensconced behind the thick walls, heavy wooden doors and wrought iron gates typical of early Dutch craftsmanship. It now contains the Malacca Historical Museum, tracing the history of the state. Among the collections are displays of traditional Chinese and Malay wedding costumes. *Open:* daily 09.00–17.00 hrs, except Fridays. Admission free.

◆◆◆
TRADITIONAL MALACCAN HOUSES

These traditional structures are well worth hunting out. Some of the finest are seen along Jalan Bandar Hilir and its continuation, Jalan Ujong Pasir. The basic design features steeply pitched roofs, low wooden verandahs and *anjongs* (porches). Beautifully carved gables are seen on some houses, while others are entered up ornately tiled steps.

Accommodation

Malacca offers many moderately priced hotels, and there are also beach resorts, chalets and bungalows available in and around Melaka town. Bookings are advisable.
Malacca Village Resort, Ayer

Keroh (tel: (06) 323600). Located near Ayer Keroh golf course, a 20-minute drive from Melaka town. 146 rooms; Asian, Continental and Chinese menus. Swimming-pool. Horse-cart and pony rides. Popular with local families. Moderate.

Merlin Inn, Jalan Bendahara (tel: (06) 240777). 225 rooms. Comfortable. Cheap.

Mid-Town Hotel, 20 Jalan Tun Sri Lanang (tel: (06) 240088). 84 basic rooms. Cheap.

Ramada Renaissance, Jalan Bendahara (tel: (06) 248888). 295 rooms with air-conditioning, TV. Three restaurants, two bars, swimming-pool, health and business centre. Moderate to expensive.

A shuttered house in the traditional Malay style

Nightlife
Melaka is on the quiet side after dark, though tourist hotels such as the Ramada Renaissance have discothèques and the downtown karaoke bars are popular. There is a *Son et Lumière* at Bandar Hilir's Padang Pahlawan. Check with the Malacca Tourist Information Centre at Jalan Kota (tel: (06) 236538) for details.

Restaurants
Melaka has a reputation for delicious cuisine, so although Western food is served in tourist hotels, do not miss an opportunity of trying local dishes. This is where to taste Nonya dishes, the distinctive Straits Chinese cuisine. Look out for *Ole Sayang* and *Nonya Makko* restaurants which specialise in Nonya food. For a taste of authentic Malay cuisine try **Restoran Anda** (tel: 231984), **Melati Lounge** (tel: 227959) or **Sri Percik**. Any taxi-driver will know the location. Glutton's Corner along Jalan Taman, Bandar Hilir, is a popular local eating spot, where hawker stalls serve a variety of Chinese, Malay and Indian foods at rock bottom prices. Serkam (6 miles/10km from Melaka) is reputed for seafood.

Shopping
Melaka offers a choice of shopping complexes on Jalan Munshi Abdullah, Jalan Bunga Raya and Jalan Bendahara. Some picturesque old streets such as Jalan Hang Jebat specialise in reasonably-priced antiques. If you find a genuine antique item, it is essential to obtain an export licence.

WHAT TO SEE IN MALACCA

Travelling by ox-cart is an experience unique to Malacca

◆◆
MALACCA REPTILE PARK
7 miles (11km) from Melaka
There are more than a thousand snakes in the park from 30 different species. Star attraction is the poisonous yellow cobra. Children also enjoy the aquaria, carp pond and rabbit garden. Refreshments and WC.
Open: daily 09.00–19.00 hrs. Admission charge.

◆◆◆
MERLIMAU
18 miles (27km) southeast of Melaka
Near Merlimau, almost on the state border with Johor, take the Muar road for a chance to see an exceptional 19th-century Malaccan-style house. Its stairway and porch are richly embellished with colourful, hand-painted tiles.

◆
MINI-MALAYSIA
7½ miles (12km) north of Melaka
If you have seen the Karyaneka in Kuala Lumpur you can skip this although the setting is better. Mini-Malaysia depicts the traditional architecture of the 13 states. Each house contains works of art and crafts from the relevant state. In addition, there are weekly cultural shows and traditional games.
Open: Monday to Friday 10.00–18.00 hrs, and Saturday to Sunday 09.00–19.00 hrs. Admission free.

STATE OF NEGERI SEMBILAN

Negeri Sembilan is just an hour's drive from Kuala Lumpur, and coastal towns, such as Port Dickson, are a popular weekend retreat from the capital for many Malay families. Local houses are characterised by sweeping, horn-shaped roofs reflecting the early influence of Minangkabau settlers from the Indonesian island of Sumatra. Rubber and palm oil are important local crops and handicrafts and curios a speciality.

SEREMBAN

The state capital, Seremban, is a moderate-sized community with scores of cheap, Chinese-owned hotels, though few foreign visitors stay. Local food is good, however, and a lunchtime stop is recommended. Strolling around the town, keep a look out for the striking Minangkabau-style roof topping the State Legislature Council Building, and the elegant, colonial-style State Library dating from 1912.

WHAT TO SEE

◆
TAMAN BUNGA (LAKE GARDENS)
These attractive gardens occupy a long, narrow valley stretching southeast of Seremban city centre. The State Mosque overlooks the gardens, its nine pillars representing the nine original districts of Negeri Sembilan (Nine States). The **Bird Park** is another popular attraction.

◆◆
TAMAN SENI BUDAYA (CULTURAL COMPLEX)
1¾ miles (3km) from Seremban on the Expressway to KL
Situated near the 60km point of the Expressway, the complex is devoted to displays of Malay arts, and contains several important buildings. On the ground floor of the main building, **Terapak Perpatih**, exhibits include examples of various crafts such as woodcarving, pottery and batik. The spectacular roof is a fine example of traditional Minangkabau architecture. The **State Museum** is here. Built in 1861, this former royal residence was dismantled in 1953, and transported piece by piece to Seremban. More recently, it was moved again to its present site. Another fine old wooden building, the **Rumah Contoh Minangkabau**, was originally built for a Malay prince. The house was shipped to England and exhibited as an example of Malay architecture in 1924. Reassembled near the State Museum, it is occasionally used for displays of martial arts, dancing and top-spinning. *Open:* Saturday to Wednesday 09.00–18.00 hrs, and Thursday mornings. Admission free.

Food and Drink
Dishes are heavily spiced and liberally laced with chilli. Look out for street vendors preparing *lemang* (sticky rice) which is cooked on bamboo by the roadside (as in Terengganu). Good Malay restaurants in town are the **Flamingo Inn, Fatimah Restaurant** and **Bilal**.

WHAT TO SEE IN NEGERI SEMBILAN

◆
PEDAS HOT SPRINGS
18½ miles (30km) southeast of Seremban
A popular local attraction with bathing facilities, the hot springs can get crowded at weekends. Refreshments and WC available.

◆◆◆
PORT DICKSON
20 miles (32km) south of Seremban
Pleasant old resort town with a long, sandy beach and safe bathing. The **Yacht Club** (4½ miles/7km outside town) is a popular weekend rendezvous for Westerners with swimming-pool and tennis courts. Members can recommend guests. Despite development, the town remains unspoilt and offers a wide choice of reasonably-priced small hotels. Waterskiing, windsurfing and fishing trips are easily arranged; outboards can be rented from beachside hotels.

STATE OF PAHANG

Tourism in Pahang is centred on the east coast, near the capital Kuantan, and in the cool hill stations in west Pahang. Kuantan is the biggest town. Driving up the coast, towards Kuala Terengganu, you pass lovely palm-lined beaches washed by the South China Sea. Typical Malay *kampungs* line the roadside. The population is mainly Malay and comprises farmers and fishermen. The state has well developed natural resources such as rubber and palm oil. Cocoa and copra are also important crops; and tourist interest has boosted local cottage industries such as weaving and painting. Two-thirds of Pahang is rain forest. It encloses the vast **Taman Negara** (National Park), which extends into Kelantan and Terengganu. Pahang has a similar hot and humid climate to other states in West Malaysia. The wet season between

On the river near Kuantan

November and January should be avoided.

KUANTAN

At the mouth of the Kuantan river, the state capital offers little in the way of tourist attractions. It is, however, a good base from which to explore part of the east coast, and an important transport terminal. In the town there are some old-style shop-houses along Jalan Besar, near the Taman Seni Budaya Cultural Centre. Otherwise, the heart of the city is modern, characterised by a prosperous business centre and the multi-storey Terentum Shopping Kompleks.

Accommodation

There are plenty of cheap Chinese-operated hotels in central Kuantan, but the discerning traveller heads for the beach hotels at Teluk Cempedak (3 miles/5km), and the coastal village of Beserah, just 2½ miles (4km) north of the city.

Coral Beach Resort, 152 Sungai Karang, Beserah (tel: (09) 587544). 162 rooms, including 78 de luxe with sea view, 15 minutes from Kuantan. Moderate.

Gloria Maris Resort, Mastura 1/1402, Kg Bahru Beserah (tel: (09) 587788). Simple timber chalets on beach, some with air-conditioning, fridge and TV. A good base for local sightseeing. Cheap.

Hyatt Kuantan, PO Box 140, Teluk Cempedak (tel: (09) 525211). 185 beachside rooms with air-conditioning, international direct dialling, TV, balcony and mini-bar. Two minutes' drive from

18-hole Royal Pahang Golf Course. Children's centre with baby-sitters. Expensive.

Merlin Inn Resort, PO Box 46, Teluk Cempedak (tel: (09) 511388). 106 rooms with all amenities. Watersports facilities and indoor games. Moderate to expensive.

Nightlife

Kuantan's nightlife is pretty limited and designed to appeal to local Chinese. There is a karaoke lounge at Teluk Cempedak, but social life centres on the Hyatt's verandah bar and discothèque. The hotel also stages theme evenings with traditional dancing and a weekly Pasar Malam (night market).

Restaurants

Kuantan has a generous complement of good Chinese and seafood restaurants, and Western food is widely available in tourist hotels. **Restaurant Din**, at Teluk Cempedak, is particularly recommended for seafood and Malay-style cuisine.

Shopping

Village crafts make attractive souvenirs. The Tourist Office in Kuantan has a gift shop, and there are numerous beachside stalls selling carvings and jewellery and other handicrafts. Further afield, check out the craft scene at **Balok** and **Beserah**, where local women make Malay dolls, shellwork objects, woven mats and driftwood artefacts. There is a craftwork centre in **Kampung Cherating**, and batik is sold everywhere. Visitors to the Cameron Highlands usually stock up on local tea and coffee.

WHAT TO SEE IN EAST PAHANG

◆
BESERAH
2½ miles (4km) north of Kuantan
Best known for its dried salted fish, and the pungent fish paste called *belacan*, this coastal *kampung* also boasts a thriving craft industry producing attractive carvings and excellent batik prints. The fishing boats return around midday and the catch is transported to the village in carts pulled by water buffalo. Good Wednesday night market from 17.00 hrs.

◆◆
KAMPUNG BALOK
11 miles (18km) north of Kuantan
This long, sandy beach makes a good excursion. There is excellent windsurfing here, and a chance to buy some of the local crafts in the village.

◆
KAMPUNG CHENDOR
32 miles (52km) north of Kuantan
Almost on the border with the neighbouring state of Terengganu, this popular local picnic spot draws fascinated onlookers when the turtles come ashore to breed during May to October. There is a good motel and youth hostel.

◆◆
KAMPUNG CHERATING
29 miles (47km) from Kuantan
Cherating is the idyllic site of Southeast Asia's first Club Méditerranée. If you are not staying, the Club has a day membership rate which allows visitors to use all facilities. Good swimming from the fabulous beach and a tempting local handicrafts centre.

◆◆
PEKAN
27 miles (44km) south of Kuantan
The royal town of Pahang was once the state capital, but now rests quietly on the banks of the Pahang River. Pekan still houses the State Museum and its fine collections of crafts and historical artefacts. The **Istana Abu Bakar** (Royal Palace) is flanked by a polo field, which occasionally sees service as a golf course. And there is a silk-weaving centre well worth a visit at **Pulau Keladi** (3 miles/ 5km).

◆◆◆
TAMAN NEGARA
A vast national park in the heart of Pahang's tropical forest-land, Taman Negara can offer boating, jungle walks along well-marked trails and climbing opportunities. Arrangements to visit the park must be made in advance through the Department of Wildlife and National Parks in Kuala Lumpur (tel: (03) 9052872). The park is closed 15 November to 14 January. (See **Peace and Quiet**, page 91.)

◆
TASEK (LAKE) CHINI
62 miles (100km) inland from Kuantan
This popular excursion has jungle walks and lovely views over the lake, which is carpeted with lotus blossoms from June to September. Basic accommodation is available, including camp sites.

Tea estate, Cameron Highlands

WHAT TO SEE IN WEST PAHANG: THE HILL RESORTS

Log fires and cream teas are not usually associated with Asia, but Malaysia's hill resorts developed by the British retain a distinctly colonial atmosphere. Country-style hotels are planted on misty mountain foothills, where visitors can sleep under blankets and swing a golf-club without sweating. It is an invigorating change from the coastal heat. Even the landscape is softer on the eye, with tea and coffee estates replacing rubber and palm oil.

◆◆◆
CAMERON HIGHLANDS

205 miles (330km) north of KL
Named for British surveyor, William Cameron, who discovered the area in 1885, the hills were settled by 19th-century tea-planters and Chinese market gardeners. Seeking a cool weekend retreat, civil servants followed. They created a corner of rural England in Asia, which continues to delight present-day visitors.

Cameron Highlands is made up of three small townships. Driving up the winding mountain road from Tapah (off the KL–Ipoh road), the first township is **Ringlet**, a supply

town of no lasting interest. Fruit, vegetables and flowers are grown on farms lining the roads. First planted in 1926, tea is now an established industry.
Tanah Rata lies eight miles (13km) on from Ringlet. It is the biggest town and the most suitable base, with several shops, a launderette, a post office and an ITT phonecard box. There is a Hong Kong & Shanghai Bank, as well as a money changer (beside Restaurant No 14). Transit hotels in the area all have restaurants (see **Accommodation**, page 47); backpackers congregate in the **Mayflower, Thanam** and **Kumar** restaurants.
The highland climate is capricious. Wet, misty mornings suddenly clear to blue skies, but be prepared to wrap up as soon as the sun sets. Take rainwear and comfortable walking shoes. A favourite outing (by taxi or on foot) from Tanah Rata is the town of **Berinchang**. Built on a

See the leaves being dried on a visit to one of the tea factories

hill around a square, Berinchang has hotels, shops, and a karaoke lounge for entertainment. Beyond Berinchang, numerous tracks lead to lofty peaks: the highest is Gunung Berinchang. There are several other gentle walks around Tanah Rata, including jaunts to the **Robinson Waterfall**, and the **Parit Waterfall**. Serious hill walkers and climbers can obtain further information from the Fraser's Hill Tourist Office. A visit to a tea estate is highly recommended. The **Blue Valley, Boh Tea Gunong Emas** and **Sungei Palas Tea** estates are all conveniently close. An outing to Boh Tea includes a lovely winding drive through lush hillside, a conducted tour, and the chance to stock up on local produce from the small gift shop. Gardeners might enjoy an inspection of the flower nurseries. Try the ones situated on the main road, near The Lakehouse hotel. Fishermen with tackle can join local anglers fishing for carp on the **Sultan Abu Bakar Dam**, situated at Km51 on the trunk road. Golfers should not pass up an opportunity of a round or two at the **Cameron Highlands Golf Club**.

Accommodation

There is a great variety of local accommodation, but it is in short supply. Bookings are essential during April, August and December. Two cheap hotels worth a mention are the **Federal**; and the **Town House**; both in Tanah Rata town centre. **The Lakehouse**, 30th Mile, Ringlet (tel: (05) 996152). 16 rooms in 'English' country hotel on a hill overlooking the lake. Comfortable base. Western food. Moderate to expensive. **Kowloon Hotel**, 34–45 Berinchang (tel: (05) 941366). 12 rooms in the town centre. Chinese/Western cuisine and licensed bar. Central walking base. Cheap. **Merlin Inn Resort**, Tanah Rata (tel: (05) 941211). 64 rooms in tourist-style hotel. Tennis courts, near golf course, bicycles for hire. Chinese, Western and Malay cuisine. Quiet. Moderate. **Ye Olde Smokehouse**, Berinchang/Tanah Rata (tel: (05) 941214/5). 20 rooms in a charming 'English' country hotel planted in luxuriant gardens near the golf course. One of the great surprises of Malaysia. Devonshire teas; expensive restaurant. Moderate to expensive.

◆◆◆
FRASER'S HILL

62 miles (100km) north of KL
Situated 5,000 feet (1,524m) above sea-level, **Bukit Fraser** is another charming hill resort on the border with Selangor. The small township has a market, post office, general store, dispensary, launderette and cheap restaurants. You can obtain information, postcards and souvenirs from the Tourist Office. Sports facilities include tennis, a heated indoor swimming-pool, sports complex with a gym and sauna and a 9-hole, par 32 golf course, which is packed during holidays. Visitors are welcome. It is an easy 3-mile (5km) walk to the **Jeriau Waterfall**; everywhere there are paths leading off the main road into the dense rainforest. Maps are available from the Fraser's Hill Development Corporation, and guides can be arranged on request.

Accommodation

There is a selection of cheap, family-style bungalows in the area. Enquiries and reservations can be made at the Fraser's Hill Information Centre (tel: (09) 382201).
Fraser's Pine Resort, Jalan Kuari (tel: (03) 7832810). 96 rooms and apartments in condominium-style complex. Sauna and games facilities. Popular with locals. Moderate.
Ye Old Smokehouse at Fraser's, on the road to Jeriau Waterfall (tel: (09) 382226). Modelled on the original in the Cameron Highlands, this attractive English-style country house

hotel was opened in 1988. Cosy atmosphere with log-fires. Quiet. Moderate to expensive.

How to Get to the Highlands

The Mara National Express bus links Kuala Lumpur with Tanah Rata (Cameron Highlands) – two buses daily each way. There are also regular buses from Kuala Lumpur (Pudu Raya Bus Terminal) to Fraser's Hill (change at Kuala Kubu Bahru). Self-drive takes about one hour from Kuala Lumpur to Kuala Kubu Bahru. From there proceed to the Gap. The last five miles (8km) are along a narrow, winding road with single lane traffic only between 06.30 and 19.00 hrs. The road is closed uphill or downhill for alternating 40-minute periods during this time.

◆
GENTING HIGHLANDS
32 miles (51km) from KL
There is a winding road up into the Gunung Ula Kali mountain range which leads to the modern hill resort town known as the Genting Highlands. Local attractions include a lake with pedal boats, horse riding, cable-car rides, a mini railway, an indoor stadium with table tennis, squash and bowling facilities, and an 18-hole golf course available to visitors at a price. Malaysia's only casino is found here too, with a choice of baccarat, blackjack, roulette, and traditional Chinese gambling games such as *keno*. The theatre restaurant, serving Chinese cuisine, can seat up to 1,200 diners. Genting Highlands operates its own air-conditioned coach service, which offers eight services daily from Pudu Raya Bus Station. The fare includes a cable-car ride. There is a wide range of accommodation. Bookings are essential, and weekends are particularly busy.

Ipoh's grand railway station

STATE OF PERAK

Perak is a pleasant, easy-going state in western Peninsular Malaysia. It contains the world's richest tin deposits, and about half its population of around two million are Chinese descendants of the original tin prospectors. Ore is obtained from granite mountain ranges extending east across the state. As well as tin, Perak is known for cave temples and fruit growing. Ipoh, the state capital, makes a comfortable overnight stop between Kuala Lumpur and Penang. Most coach tours stop only briefly, but the royal town of Kuala Kangsar is worth a one- or two-hour visit.

IPOH

Ipoh was a small market town when tin was discovered in the Kinta Valley, and its population of 4,000 in 1882 rose to 60,000 by the end of the decade. Occupying both banks of the Kinta River, 125 miles (200km) north of Kuala Lumpur, the town still boasts a considerable Chinese community with its origins in the 19th-century tin boom era. Ipoh's name derives from the *upas* tree whose poison sap was used by local aboriginal tribes to tip their poison darts. A solitary *upas* tree grows in an enclosure outside the railway station, a rather flamboyant Moorish-style structure which dates from 1917. A short distance away, several fine buildings surround the grassy *padang*, including St Michael's School and the exclusive colonial-style Royal Ipoh Club.

WHAT TO SEE

◆
GEOLOGICAL MUSEUM
Jalan Harimau
Malaysia's only geological museum displays more than 600 types of minerals, fossils and gem stones.
Open: Monday to Thursday 08.00–16.15 hrs, Friday 08.00–12.00 and 15.00–16.15 hrs, Saturday 08.00–12.45 hrs. Admission free.

◆
KELLIE'S CASTLE
on the Batu Gajah road, south of Ipoh
The unfinished dream of Scottish rubber planter William Kellie Smith, these curious ruins stand on a hill off the Ipoh-Batu Gajah back road. Kellie Smith began building in 1910, but did not survive to complete it.

◆◆
MEH PRASIT TEMPLE
Jalan Kuala Kangsar
This Thai temple on the Kuala Kangsar road houses a Buddha statue more than 80 feet (24m) long.

◆
PERAK TONG
4 miles (6km) north of Ipoh, beyond Meh Prasit Temple
Located inside a cavernous limestone cave, this temple was built in 1926 by a Buddhist monk from China. It houses 40 statues of the Buddha. The centrepiece is a 42-foot (12.8m) high statue of a sitting Buddha. Some 345 steps lead to the summit of the cave, with panoramic views. Café and WC facilities.
Open: daily. Admission by donation.

◆
TAMBUNAN (YOOK LIN) HOT SPRINGS
2 miles (3km) north of Tambunan
Hot water spas are located at the base of a limestone hill. There are changing facilities, a café and WC.
*Open:*16.00–21.00 hrs. Closed Mondays. Admission charge.

Accommodation
Royal Casuarina Hotel, 18 Jalan Gopeng (tel: (05) 505555). Tourist hotel overlooking the hills. The 200 rooms have air-conditioning, international direct dialling, mini-bar, tea/coffee making facilities. Pool, sauna, shop and beauty salon. Free airport shuttle bus. Moderate to expensive.
Station Hotel, located inside the railway station at Jalan Panglima Gantang (tel: (05) 512588). A nostalgia-inducing old imperial hotel built in 1917. Basic, but comfortable rooms with TV, mini-bar and air-conditioning. Grand long colonnaded verandah. Bar-dining room cooled by 14 ceiling fans. Cheap.

Nightlife
Downtown nightlife is local style. For a low-key night out sample the evening entertainment in the Royal Casuarina Ascot Lounge and Palm Grove discothèque.

Restaurants
For a great value three-course English meal – soup, a main course and pudding – nothing beats the menu at the **Station Hotel**. The **Garden Terrace** at the Royal Casuarina has a huge international menu and a good wine list; there is also an Italian restaurant in the hotel. **Restoran Pakeeza**, 15–17 Persiaran Green (tel: 501057), serves good, freshly prepared Mogul meals, while the **FMS Bar**, on Jalan Laksamana (opposite the *padang*), is an atmospheric, salon-style drinking hole.

Shopping
Ipoh is known for porcelain, woven crafts and bazaar-type items. The Central Market is the best place to browse.

WHAT TO SEE IN PERAK

◆◆◆
KUALA KANGSAR
31 miles (50km) north of Ipoh
Kuala Kangsar enjoys a special reverence as the royal town of Perak. First used as a royal capital in the 1740s, it is a quiet, picturesque place on the Perak River. There is no tourist-type accommodation, or restaurants. The **Muzium Diraja** (Royal Museum) is housed in the Istana Kenegan at Bukit Chandan. Built in 1926, this beautifully carved wooden building contains not a single nail. The exhibits are mainly photographs and royal regalia pertaining to the State of Perak, and the royal barge is permanently anchored alongside. Check opening times. Admission charge. Near the museum, the **Istana Iskandariah** palace is a good example of Saracenic-style architecture (entry not permitted). The other highlight of Kuala Kangsar is the magnificent **Ubidiah Mosque**. Opened for prayers in 1917, it is one of the most extravagantly designed mosques in the world.

The magnificent Ubudiah mosque

Adjacent, there are seven Royal Mausoleums honouring former Sultans of Perak. Kuala Kangsar has been renowned as the home of Malaysia's rubber industry. A huge old rubber tree in front of the local District Office is said to be one of the first planted in the country.

◆◆
LUMUT

52 miles (84km) from Ipoh
This base for the Royal Malaysian Navy is a good place to dine out on seafood. Lumut is a departure point for Pulau Pangkor (see page 52). **Teluk Batik**, a pleasant beach 3¾ miles (6km) from Lumut, offers basic chalet-type accommodation.

◆◆
PULAU PANGKOR
40-minute boat trip from Lumut (on mainland Perak)
A popular local holiday island, crowded with visitors at weekends. The resident population of around 23,000 is mainly Chinese. The most attractive fishing villages lie along the Indian Ocean coast at Pangkor. **Pasir Bogak Beach** is the largest and most popular, with camping facilities, rest-houses and changing rooms. **Teluk Nipah** is a quiet bay accessible from Pasir Bogak. Budget travellers will find cheap accommodation in the main town.

Accommodation
Pan Pacific Resort, Teluk Belanga (tel: (05) 915091). 161 rooms in tourist-style hotel, popular with local holidaymakers. Beach and swimming-pool. Expensive. **Sea View Hotel**, Pasir Bogak (tel: (05) 951605). 37 rooms near a good swimming beach. Comfortable; guests are mainly local. Cheap.

Lush Lake Gardens at Taiping

◆◆◆
TAIPING
54 miles (87km) north of Ipoh
Taiping is the tranquil old capital of Perak. The **Perak State Museum** is found here, out on Jalan Taming Sari, next to the grim Taiping Prison. It houses displays of ancient tools and weaponry, ornaments and other examples of Perak's cultural heritage. The highlight of the town is the lovely **Lake Gardens** park – 153 acres (62 hectares) of flooded tin mining excavations, landscaped with flower gardens and avenues of trees. There is a floating restaurant, children's playground and paddle-boats on the lake. The best hotel is the 70-room **Panorama**, 62–79 Jalan Kota (tel: (05) 834111). For restaurant dining, the **Restoran Air Kacang Taiping** is recommended. A six-mile (10km) drive west of Taiping, there is a mid-19th-century Malay fortress at Matang. **Kota Ngah Ibrahim** was the residence of Long Jaafar, a Malay chieftain who made his fortune with the discovery of tin in the region. Its solid appearance is testimony to the friction between rival tin mining factions.

STATE OF PERLIS

The smallest state in Malaysia is sandwiched between Kedah and the border with southern Thailand. It is picturesque and unspoilt, but few tourists venture this far north. Perlis has a hot and humid climate with a heavy rainfall between September and December. Rice, rubber and sugar cane are all important crops. The people are a mixture of Malays, Chinese, Indians and Thais. There is little Western influence and traditional pastimes remain popular.

KANGAR

The state capital of Perlis, Kangar, is a small, rather quaint town trading in agricultural goods and seafood. Transport is by bus, or shared taxi from Butterworth or Alor Setar. The International Express Train stops at Arau, six miles (10km) east of Kangar. The **State Mosque** is worth a visit; as is **Dato 'Wan Ahmad' House** on a street of the same name. Note the traditional woodcarving with painted panels and a gabled roof.

Accommodation
Pens Hotel, 135 Main Road (tel: (04) 760487). 34 rooms in a central location. Cheap.
Federal Hotel, 104 a and b Jalan Kangar (tel: (04) 766288). 48 rooms. Cheap.

Food and Drink
Without doubt, *laksa* (delicious spicy fish and coconut soup) is the most popular dish in Perlis. Try *harum manis*, a delicious locally-grown mango. There are numerous cheap Malay/Chinese/ Thai eating places. Western fare is served at the **Kangar Restaurant** in the Sri Perlis Inn and also at **Diana Fried Chicken**.

Shopping
Liu Emporium, KK Department Store and the Looking Good Centre are popular local department stores in Kangar. There is a weekly **Pasar Tani** (farmers' market) which is an interesting diversion on Saturdays. The **Pasar Malam** (night market) is on Wednesday in Kangar and Friday in Arau. **Padang Besar**, the border town with Thailand (31 miles/50km north), sells everything under the sun. The busy **Pekan Siam**, opposite the Railway Station, is a bargain-hunter's bonanza, featuring duty-free shopping, local goods and attractive imports from Thailand.

WHAT TO SEE IN PERLIS

◆
ARAU
6 miles (10km) southeast of Kangar
In the royal town of Perlis, Arau, fruit trees and palms are planted neatly between quaint houses. It is an easy place to find your way around. The main sights are the State Mosque and the Istana di-Raja, or royal palace.

◆
GUA KELAM KAKI BUKIT
16 miles (26km) from Kangar
This vast limestone cave is reached by a wooden suspension walkway above an underground stream. There is a tin mine inside the cave.

Palm trees and white sands – Penang is attainable paradise

STATE OF PULAU PINANG (PENANG)

◆◆
KUALA PERLIS
6 miles (10km) southwest of Kangar
A quaint muddle of traditional wooden fishermen's houses at the mouth of the Sungai river, Kuala Perlis is where you catch a boat to the Langkawi Islands and the Thai resort island of Phuket. The local seafood is excellent. Dine out on huge prawns, crabs and delicious *laksa*.

◆
SUNGI BATU PAHAT
6 miles (10km) from Kangar
A local picnic and recreation spot. There is a **Snake Farm** near by (*open:* Tuesday to Sunday 08.00–16.00 hrs); and a nine-hole golf course reckoned a difficult par-72.

◆
TASEK (LAKE) MELATI
5 miles (8km) from Kangar
An interesting side trip for birdwatchers. Plenty to see on this man-made lake surrounded by marshy lowland.

Pulau Pinang (Penang), capital Georgetown, consists of the island of Penang lying off the state of Kedah and a mainland coastal strip known as Province Wellesley. Covering some 110 square miles (285sq km), the island rises abruptly from palm-fringed beaches to a forested hill, 2,693 feet (821m) above sea-level. Penang has a typical equatorial climate; temperatures range between 23° and 32° C (73°–89° F), with rainfall concentrated between September and November. The population of around one million is mainly Chinese. English is widely spoken, but you will hear Chinese dialects as well as Malay, Hindu, Tamil and Thai. Highrise office blocks, hotels and condominiums indicate Penang is doing well, and it has succeeded in developing into an international tourist resort without being spoilt. Penang has everything for an excellent holiday – good beaches, world class accommodation, gourmet restaurants, a bright nightlife

and endless attractions.
Most hotels at Batu Ferringhi
offer special children's
facilities such as wading pool,
games room and baby-sitting
facilities. Penang is easily
accessible with direct links
from Bangkok, Singapore and,
via Kuala Lumpur, with London,
Los Angeles and Sydney. MAS
operate 24 flights daily from
Kuala Lumpur. Bayan Lepas
Airport lies 12½ miles (20km)
from Georgetown. Airport taxis
have fixed fares which are
paid for at a taxi-booth in
exchange for a coupon.
Arriving by road, drivers
cross Penang Bridge from the
mainland. There is a 24-hour
ferry service from Butterworth
which does get crowded at
weekends. Holidays at
Penang's popular resorts
should be booked at least
three months in advance.

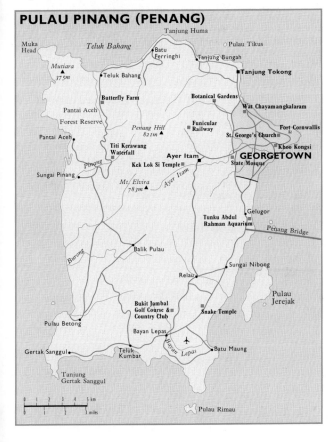

PULAU PINANG (PENANG)

GEORGETOWN

The quaint, but growing capital of Pulau Pinang, is a mixture of modern blocks piercing the skyline above the orange-tiled roofs of traditional shop-houses, but the heart of the town remains essentially Chinese. Most sights are concentrated within a square mile of the clock tower raised in memory of Queen Victoria's Diamond Jubilee. Streets are narrow, so it is best to explore by trishaw, or on foot. Drivers arriving by car should park at Fort Cornwallis, then make their way south to Lebuh Light/Light Street, lined with Victorian administrative buildings. At the harbour end is the E&O Hotel built in 1885 by the Sarkies of Raffles/Singapore fame. Five minutes' walk away is the old Protestant cemetery where the founder of Penang, Captain Francis Light, is buried. Lebuhs Leith and Muntri are characterised by traditional Chinese houses decorated with carved wooden and tiled fronts.

Craftsmen are seen working in shop-houses on Lebuh Chulia, the main thoroughfare crossing Georgetown. Rope Walk, or Jalan Pintal Tali, one of the side streets off Lebuh Chulia, boasts several interesting junk shops. Other streets specialise in Chinese herbalists whose cure-alls date back centuries. The main shopping streets are Jalan Penang and Jalan Campbell. Georgetown's

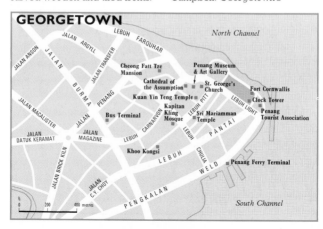

Georgetown's landmark clock tower

biggest street markets are at the junction of Jalan Penang with Jalan Campbell. (See **Shopping**, page 62.) The best time for sightseeing is before 10.00 hrs or after 16.00 hrs in the relative cool of evening. The Penang Tourist Association is found near the Clock Tower at: Street Level, PPC Building, Pesara King Edward (tel: (04) 616663).

WHAT TO SEE

◆◆◆
BATU FERRINGHI BEACH
8½ miles (14km) from Georgetown
Penang's premier beach is a long sandy strip overlooked by de luxe hotels. The swimming is excellent and there is a variety of watersports on offer. Behind the coast road are souvenir shops, money-changers, market stalls and restaurants. Batu Ferringhi remains remarkably unspoiled and is a highly recommended holiday base.

◆◆◆
BOTANICAL GARDENS
5 miles (8km) from Georgetown, off Waterfall Road
Sunk in a lush valley enclosed by jungle, the Botanical Gardens' rolling lawns are studded with palms, bamboo, ferns, ornamental ponds and flowering plants. Adjacent to the gardens is a tiny, but especially lovely palm grove. This is a pleasant spot for a picnic.

◆◆◆
BUTTERFLY FARM
12½ miles (20km) from Georgetown, near Teluk Bahang
A magical kingdom for over 1,000 butterflies from 50 different species. It is best to arrive early in the day when the butterflies are most active. Even rare types such as Rajah Brooke's Birdwing may alight on your arm. There are also scorpions on display; plus an excellent gift shop and WC facilities.
Open: Monday to Friday 09.00–17.00 hrs, Saturday, Sunday and public holidays 09.00–18.00 hrs. Admission charge.

◆◆◆
CHEONG FATT TZE MANSION
on Lebuh Leith
This is one of the rare traditional 18th-century Chinese mansions in Malaysia that is still in a habitable condition. Ancient tiled roofs, cobbled courtyards, russet brick walls, small gardens and breathtaking halls of ceremony characterise the architecture. The main hall contains the ancestral family altar. Knock and ask permission to visit – the house remains in private hands.

PENINSULAR MALAYSIA

◆◆◆
CHURCHES

There are several churches in and around Georgetown of which the two most interesting from an architectural viewpoint are St George's Anglican Church and the Roman Catholic Cathedral of the Assumption. **St George's Church**, built in 1818, is reputed to be the oldest church in Southeast Asia.

◆◆
FORT CORNWALLIS
off Jalan Fort

This is where Captain Francis Light landed on Penang in 1786. The original structure was wooden, but later rebuilt in stone and fortified with cannon by convict chain gangs in 1804–5.

◆
KAPITAN KLING MOSQUE
on Lebuh Pitt

Located in central Georgetown, the spiritual home of Penang's Indian Muslim community dates from the early 19th century. It displays typical Islamic architecture.

Open: daily, except Friday morning. Visitors must be properly attired.

◆◆◆
KEK LOK SI TEMPLE
5 miles (8km) from Georgetown at Ayer Itam

In this vast Buddhist temple, crowned by a seven-storey pagoda, the octagonal base is typically Chinese, the middle tiers are Thai and the spiral dome Burmese. The entrance resembles an Arab *souk*, lined with stalls and hustlers on either side. At the top, there is a filthy turtle pond, which symbolises long life to the Chinese. A tiring climb, but refreshments, WC and gift shop are available.

Open: daily from morning until late afternoon.

Beasts adorn the Khoo Kongsi clan house, Lebuh Cannon

◆◆◆
KHOO KONGSI (CLAN HOUSE)
in Lebuh Cannon
Founded in 1894, this splendid
temple is festooned with pillars
and carved figurines, dragons
and emblems of the Khoo family.
Open: Monday to Friday 09.00–
17.00 hrs and Saturday 09.00–
13.00 hrs. Free admission.

◆◆◆
KUAN YIN TENG TEMPLE
Jalan Masjid Kapitan Kling
Also known as the Temple of
the Goddess of Mercy, this is
the least ostentatious temple in
Georgetown.
Open: daily. Admission free.

◆◆◆
PENANG BRIDGE
Linking the island to the
mainland, this is the third
longest bridge in the world at
8.3 miles (13.5km) long.

◆◆
PENANG HILL
Penang Hill rises to 2,693 feet
(821m) above sea-level. During
the 15-minute funicular ride to
the top, the temperature can
drop to 18°C (64°F) and if
Penang is not obscured by haze,
there is a good view.

◆◆
PENANG MUSEUM AND ART
GALLERY
*on Lebuh Farquhar, next to St
George's Church*
Exhibits include old maps,
photographs and early trishaws
as well as a Chinese bridal
chamber. There is a small art
gallery on the first floor.
Open: daily 09.00–17.00 hrs.
Closed Friday 12.15–14.45 hrs.
Admission free. No
photography.

◆◆◆
SNAKE TEMPLE
*8½ miles (14km) south of
Georgetown (bus no 6)*
Built in 1850, the temple is
dedicated to the memory of a
Buddhist priest, Chor Soo Kong.
Snakes have lived in the temple
as long as anyone can recall.
Seemingly intoxicated by
burning incense, they are coiled
around the altar and the eaves.
Most are venomous pit vipers,
but those with a red spot on
their head have been defanged.
Open: daily. Admission free.

◆◆◆
SRI MARIAMMAN TEMPLE
*entrance on Lebuh Queen,
buses 1, 3, 6, 9 and 10*
Built in 1883, the temple is filled
with effigies of Hindu deities.
Among them is a statue of Lord
Subramaniam, richly embossed
with precious stones, which is
placed at the head of the local
chariot procession during
Thaipusam.
Open: daily. Admission free.

◆◆
STATE MOSQUE
*Jalan Ayer Itam and Jalan Masjid
Negeri*
It is hard to miss the mosque's
huge golden dome. Dress
appropriately. It is closed to
non-believers on Fridays.

◆◆
WAT CHAYAMANGKALARAM
on Lorong Burmah
An elaborate Buddhist temple,
the *wat* houses a huge reclining
image of the Buddha. Well over
100 feet (30m) long, it is one of
the largest of its kind in
existence. No photography. Just
opposite is the **Dhammikarama
Burmese Temple**.

◆◆
YAHONG ART GALLERY
*on Batu Ferringhi beach, near
Hotel Rasa Sayang*
Batik painting and other work
by well known artist Chuah
Thean Teng, plus fine art, crafts
and antiques from around
Malaysia and China.
Open: daily 09.30–18.30 hrs.

Round-Island Tour
It is well-worth renting a car to
spend a leisurely day looping
around the island. Allow a
minimum of three to four hours
for the round trip. From
Georgetown, starting at **Weld
Quay**, drive around Lebuh
Farquhar and out along Jalan
Northam, known as 'Millionaire's
Row' because of the palatial old
mansions. This leads to the
beach area of **Batu Ferringhi**
and **Teluk Bahang** where giant
boulders guard quiet coves.
There are three batik factories
located in the Batu Ferringhi/
Teluk Bahang area. **Craft Batik**,
signposted from Teluk Bahang,
is recommended. One of
Penang's best swimming
beaches, **Muka Head**, is
accessible by footpath from
Teluk Bahang. Head south,
passing the Forest Reserve on
your left. From here to Balik
Pulau the road winds over the
mountains and down again to
coastal paddies. There are
swimming beaches at **Pantai
Aceh**, or **Gertak Sanggul**. Both
are quiet fishing villages with
sandy beaches a short detour off
the main route. At Bayan Lepas
a road leads off to **Batu Maung**,
another fishing village with a
children's playground; and the
Bukit Jambal Golf Course and

Country Club is a delightful
18-hole course in the Bayan
Lepas area. The main road back
to Georgetown passes the
Snake Temple, and there is a
view of the new State Mosque
on the edge of town.
Budget-travellers can explore
the island by hopping on and off
the Blue and Yellow buses
which depart regularly from
Prangin Bus Terminal. It is a
very cheap mode of transport,
but the island circuit can take a
couple of days.

Accommodation
Penang is well supplied with
tourist hotels of international
standing, most of which are
grouped around the beach
resort of Batu Ferringhi.
Moderately priced hotels tend
to be in Georgetown.
City Bayview, 25A Lebuh
Farquhar, Georgetown (tel: (04)
363161). A well-run, friendly
hotel with 160 rooms and
excellent views of Penang. Pool
and health club. Moderate.
E&O/Eastern and Oriental, 10
Lebuh Farquhar, (tel: (04)
635322). Old-style hotel living off
its reputation. 100 rooms, large,
airy and comfortable, but slack
service. Dress for dinner.
Moderate.
Equatorial Hotel, 1 Jalan Bukit
Jambal, Bayan Lepas (tel: (04)
838111). 415 rooms, five minutes
from the airport. Adjoining
18-hole golf course; French,
Japanese and Chinese
restaurants. A first-class tourist
hotel with all facilities.
Moderate.
Holiday Inn, Batu Ferringhi (tel:
(04) 811601). 152 rooms
overlooking the beach. First

The luxurious Penang Mutiara

class facilities, including watersports and Continental dining. Moderate.

Lone Pine Hotel, 97 Batu Ferringhi (tel: (04) 811511). 54 air-conditioned rooms in comfortable, quiet beachfront hotel. Recommended. Cheap.

Parkroyal, Batu Ferringhi (tel: (04) 811133). New 333-room hotel facing the beach. First class facilities; good for families – no extra charge for children under 14 sharing with parents.

Penang Mutiara, 1 Jalan Teluk Bahang, Batu Ferringhi (tel: (04) 812828). On a beachfront site with all watersports. 440 de luxe rooms with balcony, sea view, kingsize baths and separate shower. Coffee shop and four restaurants serving Western, Continental, Chinese, Japanese and local cuisine. Shopping arcade, business centre and gym. Good evening entertainments. Expensive but highly recommended.

Rasa Sayang, Batu Ferringhi (tel: (04) 811811). 320 rooms in superior beachfront hotel. Large pool and garden area. Gym, sailing, windsurfing, waterskiing

and paragliding available. Western, Malay and Japanese cuisine, plus good seafood; 24-hour coffee-house. Expensive.

Tye Anne Hotel, 285 Lebuh Chulia, Georgetown (tel: (04) 614875). A small, clean, simple hotel-café greatly loved by backpackers. Dormitory accommodation or single rooms, communal WC/bath. Very cheap.

Nightlife

Penang has a bright, if not exactly decadent nightlife centred mainly in the Batu Ferringhi beach district. Favourite discothèques include the high-tech **Study** in the Penang Mutiara; the **Betel Nut** disco-pub, opposite the Holiday Inn; the **Fun Club** in the Golden Sands Hotel; and the Parkroyal's **Borsalino**. Neon signs indicate bars and karaoke lounges in and around Georgetown. For a change of tempo, there is old-time dancing at the venerable E&O Hotel.

The beach at Batu Ferringhi

Restaurants

Penang is an island that lives to eat. The seafood is superb and local Chinese restaurants are among the best in Malaysia. There is an enormous choice of eateries from the elegant ambience of **Eden Village** (tel: 811852) to the cheap and cheerful delights of hawker stalls. There is no shortage of variety – *sotong, laksa,* prawn *mee* and *rojak* salad are all worth trying. Be adventurous. As well as Chinese, Nonya and Malay food, there are Italian, Indian and Japanese restaurants on the island. The **Shin Miyako** (tel: 368702), in Penang Road, serves good value Japanese cuisine; while **Tandoori House** (tel: 619105) is a well-established Georgetown Mogul restaurant. Hotels on Batu Ferringhi offer a broad choice of Western, Asian and seafood dishes. **The Catch** (tel: 812828), a live seafood restaurant in the Penang Mutiara, is recommended. **Happy Garden** (tel: 811199) is a popular, small restaurant also located at Batu Ferringhi. The village of Batu Maung is famous for its seafood – try the local chilli crab.

Shopping

Penang offers the best shopping in Malaysia after Kuala Lumpur. Georgetown's air-conditioned shopping complexes, such as **Komtar, Yaohan, Gama** and **Super-Burmah** are a great place to browse and enjoy a snack, or drink, in the fresh food bars. There are numerous boutiques, also specialist shops selling pewterware, ceramics and antiques. The main shopping streets are Jalan Penang and Jalan Campbell. The **Chowrasta Market** and **Piccadilly Bazaar** sell everything under the sun; and the **Pasar Malam** (night market) is also packed with bargains. After sundown, hawker stalls set up along Batu Ferringhi beach. They are good for cassettes and fake watches. Bargaining is expected. Duty-free items such as cameras and pens are cheap. Visitors to Batu Ferringhi could try **Sriwani Tax-Free Emporium**, near the Palm Beach Hotel. **Craft Batik** and the **Penang Butterfly Farm** both have excellent gift shops. Most shops open from 09.00–20.00 hrs, or later.

STATE OF SELANGOR

The densely populated and industrialised state of Selangor surrounds the federal capital. Port Kelang is Malaysia's biggest port, and Kuala Lumpur/ Subang International Airport lies within Selangor. It is said of Selangor that every road ends in a rubber plantation, though tin was important in the early days. The Sultanate of Selangor was established in the 18th century by Bugis traders from Indonesia. Fighting between Bugis, Malays and rival factions of Chinese tin miners obliged the sultan to accept a British resident in 1874.

SHAH ALAM

The capital of Selangor, Shah Alam is conveniently located between Kuala Lumpur and Pelabuhan (Port) Kelang. A modern, industrialised town, it boasts some striking state-of-the-art architecture. Landmarks include the stunning State Secretariat Building, together with the Museum. Town Hall, Library and Conference Centre. However, the highlight is the **Sultan Salahuddin Abdul Shah Mosque**, which dominates the heart of Shah Alam. A blend of traditional Islamic and Malay architecture, the dazzling blue dome covers a prayer-hall which can accommodate 10,000 worshippers. The *mihrab* (a niche in the prayer-hall indicating the direction of Mecca) is made of marble and antique Turkish tiles. Entry is restricted to visitors who are properly attired and women who are not menstruating. *Open:* to non-Muslims Monday to Thursday 09.00–12.00 and 14.00–16.00 hrs, Saturday and Sunday 17.00–18.30 hrs.

The best way to get around is by car. The Kuala Lumpur–Kelang bus service (no 22) stops at Shah Alam. Taxi fares from KL should be agreed in advance.

Tapping for rubber in Selangor

Accommodation

There are several fine local hotels.

Holiday Inn Shah Alam, Plaza Peransang, Persiaran Perbandaran, Shah Alam (tel: (03) 5503696). 154 rooms; first class facilities aimed at the travelling businessman rather than tourists. Expensive.

Hyatt Saujana, PO Box 111, Subang International Airport Highway, Petaling Jaya (tel: (03) 7461188). 230 rooms with TV, international direct dialling, mini-bar. Peaceful location next to an 18-hole championship golf course. Convenient for the airport. Highly recommended. Expensive.

Restaurants

The cheapest and most popular eating places in Selangor are roadside hawkers, who offer a full range of Malay, Chinese and Indian dishes cooked while you wait. Selangor's international hotels serve Western food ranging from pizza to steak. The **Suria Café** in the Hyatt Saujana specialises in authentic Nonya cuisine at moderate prices.

Shopping

An excellent local purchase is pewter from the **Selangor Pewter Factory** (see page 66). The **Selayang Batik Factory**, on the road to Batu Caves, specialises in handmade and block-printed textiles (*open:* Monday to Friday 09.00–14.00 hrs and Saturday until 13.00 hrs). An unusual souvenir is a mounted insect – a spider, scorpion or butterfly. The best place for these is **Syarikat Papillon**, 14 Lorong Perusahaan Rengan Satu (near the Batu Caves).

WHAT TO SEE IN SELANGOR

♦♦♦
BATU CAVES

8 miles (13 km) north of KL

These colossal limestone formations were discovered by an American naturalist in 1878. Subsequent exploration revealed rare species of flora typical of the 120 million-year-old caves. Malaysia's Hindu community have found the caves an appropriate place of worship. It is a stiff climb up 272 steps to the cave entrance. The best known of three main caves accessible to visitors is the Art Gallery Cave (small entrance fee). The interior is decorated with fanciful representations of Hindu deities and other lively creatures from Hindu mythology. The Temple Cave is an awesome cavern with a vaulted ceiling reaching 330 feet (100m) above the ground. During the Thaipusam festival, as many as 80,000 Hindu

devotees throng the cave. As penance, many carry *kavadis*, decorated frames with hooks and skewers used to pierce the skin, nipples and tongue. Snack and soft drinks stands are in the parking area. The caves are very busy at weekends. Access from Kuala Lumpur by Len Omnibus numbers 69 and 70 and mini-bus number 11.
Open: daily 07.00–21.00 hrs.

◆
KELANG
20 miles (32km) west of KL
The old capital of Selangor, overlooking the Kelang river, Kelang's historic landmarks are the fort, and a former storehouse, recently restored to house a small museum. From Kelang, there are ferry boats to Pulau Ketam (Crab Island), a fishing village built on stilts. Picturesque in an endearingly scruffy way, it is crowded at weekends.

◆◆
KUALA SELANGOR
40 miles (65km) northwest of KL
The former royal town of Kuala Selangor lies in the estuary of the Selangor River. The main sight is **Bukit Melawati**, the ruins of a Dutch-Malay fort with fine old cannons, and good views. On the accommodation front there is a small rest-house. Outdoor activities include trips to Pulau Angsa (6 miles/10km offshore) for bird-watching and fishing. Take a picnic. Or there is the excellent **Kuala Selangor Nature Park**, a 1,580-acre (640-hectare) area of coastal swampland which is home to around 130 species of birds. There is a Visitor's Information Centre at Bukit Melawati, paths through the mangrove forest, and observation hides. Accessible by bus from Kelang and the Pudu Raya bus terminal in Kuala Lumpur.

Lord Vishnu in the Batu caves

◆
MIMALAND
11 miles (18km) north of KL
A popular local recreation park and resort with the largest swimming-pool in the country and giant waterslides. The park is usually noisy and crowded with Malay families.

◆◆◆
SELANGOR PEWTER FACTORY
4 Jalan Usahawan Enam, Setapak Jaya (north of KL)
A 30-minute drive from central Kuala Lumpur, the Selangor Pewter Factory combines sightseeing and shopping. It employs 700 craftsmen who make beautiful pewterware objects by hand. There are guided tours of the factory. Outside the showroom the world's biggest beer tankard weighs in at 3,433 pounds (1,557kg) and has a volume capacity of 613 gallons (2,790 litres). The showroom exhibits over 600 objects including tableware, picture frames, lighters and desk sets.
Open: Monday to Friday 08.30–17.00 hrs.

◆◆
SOCFIN HOUSE
½ mile (1km) from Batang Berjuntai on the B33 north of KL
This splendid old-style European planter's bungalow is the property of the Socfin company who pioneered oil palm planting in Malaysia. Near the Selangor river, the closest town is Batang Berjuntai, famous for an attractive Hindu temple.

◆
TEMPLER PARK
13½ miles (20km) north of KL
The park is named after its founder, Sir Gerald Templer, the last British High Commissioner in Malaya. Its 1,230 acres (500 hectares) of natural forest are rich in typical flora and fauna. Forest walks lead past cascades and natural rock pools. On the edge of the park is Bukit Takun, a lofty, razor-edged limestone pinnacle. Climbers should not attempt it without an experienced local guide.

◆◆
ZOO NEGARA (NATIONAL ZOO) AND AQUARIUM
8 miles (13km) northeast of KL
The National Zoo is home to some 200 species of exotic local mammals and birds. Its large reptile house and aquarium boast over 80 species of marine and freshwater fish. Do not miss the killer toman, or giant snakehead *(Channa micropeltes)*.
Open: daily 09.00–18.00 hrs, including holidays. Admission fee and additional camera charge.

Pewter is an excellent souvenir

STATE OF TERENGGANU

The northeastern state of Terengganu is picture postcard Malaysia. The coast is fringed with sandy beaches and coconut palms. Rantau Abang is one of only six beaches in the world where leatherback turtles lay their eggs. The majority of the Malay population lives in quiet fishing villages spread around looking-glass lagoons. While not as strict as the neighbouring Muslim state of Kelantan, the local people hold conservative views. Fishing and farming are traditional activities in Terengganu, but offshore oil now provides the main state income. Tourism is underdeveloped. There is only one Western-type resort, at Tanjung Jara. Elsewhere the countryside remains rustic – wherein lies its charm. Terengganu is where travellers can unwind and enjoy outdoor activities. Traditional leisure pursuits such as kite-flying and top-spinning retain their popularity. The state is reputed for local handicrafts, particularly batik and songket. Travellers should stock up on essential supplies as there are few shops outside Kuala Terengganu.

KUALA TERENGGANU

The state capital, Kuala Terengganu, is rather down at heel. Its once picturesque old Chinese shop-houses with their long, sloping roofs are in need of paint. Sights such as the waterfront market area, the new administrative centre, the former sultan's palace, Istana Maziah, and Chinatown can be seen in a morning. Jalan Bandar has some interesting Chinese shops. Ferries link the town with **Pulau Duyong**, a boat-building island in the river estuary, where local craftsmen, using no plans, build yachts for international clients. Kuala Terengganu's market sells an abundance of seafood: prawns, lobsters, crabs and fish. Get there early before it starts to smell.

Accommodation

Places to stay are limited; if you must stay in town, try:
Pantai Primula Hotel, Jalan Persinggahan (tel: (09) 622100). A half mile (1km) south of town. Hideous architecture, but the 264 air-conditioned rooms have international direct dialling and TV. Swimming-pool and beach. Good Chinese restaurant. Moderate.

Nightlife

The Pantai Primula Hotel has a Western-type discothèque with an uncompromising sign stating 'Male to Male Dancing NOT Allowed'. Downtown there are local-type music lounges. At weekends there may be traditional dancing at the **Gelanggang Seni** cultural centre.

Restaurants

Kuala Terengganu has many good Hokkien Chinese restaurants and cheap seafood outlets. The **Pantai Restaurant** on Jalan Sultan Zainal Abidin has a good reputation. Malaysian meals are served at the **Taman Selera** in Pantai Batu Buruk. There are one or two Western-style fast food outlets.

Shopping

For arts and crafts, visit the brassware and batik workshops in **Kampung Ladang**. A songket workshop is located on Jalan Kenanga, and songket weaving is also done in **Kampung Pulau Pusa** (accessible by boat, or bus). Most local handicrafts are offered for sale in the **Karyaneka Handicraft Centre** at Kampung Rusila. Look out for the small shop situated on the right side of the road eight miles (13km) south of Kuala Terengganu.

WHAT TO SEE IN TERENGGANU

KAMPUNG MERANG

10½ miles (17km) south of Kuala Terengganu. Turn right off Route T1

One of the most picturesque fishing villages on the east coast, Kampung Merang lies just off Route T1. To reach the *kampung* visitors must take the bridge across the lagoon. There are plenty of shady picnic spots and good, safe swimming. Several simple guesthouses on the hillside opposite are ideal for backpackers. Or try the **Island View Resort**, Lot 1507, Jalan Bukit Batu Merah, Kampung Merang (tel: (09) 682006). It is rustic, friendly and cheap, with a boat service to the offshore islands.

PULAU KAPAS

a 30-minute boat trip from Merang

A good spot for quiet, unspoilt beaches, swimming and diving. There is basic accommodation in A-frames at the grandly named Kapas Island Resort (tel: (09) 68259). Cheap.

PULAU PERHENTIAN

13 miles (21km) off Kampung Kuala Besut (67 miles/108km) north of Kuala Terengganu

Kampung Kuala Besut is a dreary fishing town on the mouth of the Besut river, near the border with Kelantan. However, the Fisheries Complex is the departure point for boats to Pulau Perhentian, part of the Terengganu Marine Park (together with Kapas, Redang and Tenggol Islands). A lush, tropical island, Perhentian has beautiful quiet beaches and good diving off its coral reefs. Divers will need their own equipment; the best diving time is May to October, when the visibility is good. The **Perhentian Island Resort** (tel: (09) 2438011), offers comfortable thatched chalets and basic A-frame huts. There are also 23 campsites on the island. Travellers stranded in Besut will find 35 rooms in the comfortable but uninspiring **Primula Beach Resort**, Pantai Peranginan Air Tawar (tel: (09) 9763111), half a mile (1km) south of the bridge into Besut.

PULAU REDANG

1hr by boat from Kampung Merang

Divers reckon Redang is one of the best spots in Malaysia. Facilities are very limited. Camping only. There is one small fishing village which sells soft drinks – take any other supplies.

◆◆
RANTAU ABANG TURTLE SANCTUARY
35 miles (56km) south of Kuala Terengganu
An interesting overnight stop between May and September when giant leatherback turtles lumber on to the beach to lay their eggs. There is open beach access during the day, but low-cost tickets are required for night viewing in semi-public areas – available from local guides. Flashlight photography is forbidden; take a torch. There is a **Turtle Information Centre** further down the road.
Open: daily June to August 10.00–23.00 hrs; September to May Saturday to Thursday during office hours.

Accommodation
There are several guesthouses along the main coast road, also: **Rantau Abang Visitor Centre**, Kuala Dungun (tel: (09) 844169). 10 timber chalets set amid lush tropical foliage near Kuala Dungun, close to the turtle-laying beach. Swimming.

Traditional life is unchanged in many Malay coastal villages

◆
SEKAYU WATERFALLS
35 miles (56km) southwest of Kuala Terengganu
The waterfalls are located in a recreational forest park, and reached by a one-mile (1.5km) uphill walk. The site has shelters, changing rooms, WC facilities and chalets. There are campsites across the river. It is a popular attraction at weekends. A small fee is charged per vehicle upon entry.

◆◆
SUTERASEMAI SILK CENTRE
at Kuala Ibai, 3½ miles (6km) south of Kuala Terengganu
This silk centre is said to be the largest enterprise of its type in the world. Visitors can see every aspect of silk production from planting the mulberry trees, through harvesting, weaving and printing to the finished article.
Check opening times.

Lake Kenyir is best explored by boat, cheaper during midweek

◆◆◆
TANJUNG JARA
39 miles (64km) south of Kuala Terengganu
Blessed with a lovely beachside location, Tanjung Jara is probably the best base for exploring the east coast, with a choice of local expeditions to *kampungs* and the turtle beach at Rantau Abang, plus boat-trips up the Sungei Dungun river, or to Pulau Tenggol (13½ miles/ 22km offshore).

Accommodation
Tanjung Jara Beach Resort, 5 miles (8km) north of Kuala Dungun (tel: (09) 841801). 100 spacious rooms with separate dressing-rooms, refrigerator, air-conditioning. Suites are built on wooden stilts overlooking a lagoon. Excellent beach with windsurfing, sailing, waterskiing and snorkelling. Tennis, squash and cycling facilities. Excellent for families – children's swimming-pool. Highly recommended. Moderate to expensive.

◆
TASEK (LAKE) KENYIR
34 miles (55km) west of Kuala Terengganu
Keen fishermen will find this large dam on the Terengganu river a worthwhile detour. Kenyir is an angler's paradise. Some 40 species of fish inhabit the lake including the giant toman *(Channa micropeltes)*, also known as a snakehead. Of piranha-type disposition, the toman attacks viciously: swimming in Kenyir Lake is forbidden.

There are boats for rent by the car park; rates are exorbitant at weekends when Kenyir is visited by local families. There are no tackle shops, so arrive equipped with fishing gear. An Information Centre sells soft drinks, and displays a handy poster identifying the various fish. There is chalet-type accommodation at **Kenyir Lake Resort** (tel: (01) 950609).

EAST MALAYSIA

STATE OF SABAH

Sabah occupies the northern tip of Borneo. Its southern border is shared with Malaysia's other eastern state Sarawak, and the Indonesian state of Kalimantan. A mountainous country, Sabah boasts Gunung (Mount) Kinabalu, the highest peak in Southeast Asia at 13,450 feet (4,101m). The climate varies from a coastal temperature of around 30°C (85°F) to 18°C (64°F) on Gunung Kinabalu. Though sea breezes temper the humidity, Sabah lies outside the typhoon belt and for this reason is known as 'The Land Below the Wind'. The best time to visit is between April and October. The main towns are linked to the capital, Kota Kinabalu, by daily flights. Road-building is a battle through swamps and rainforest. Sealed roads connect most towns; elsewhere are gravel tracks. Sabah State Railways operates from Tanjung Aru (Kota Kinabalu's beach area) to Tenom. Local boats go to offshore islands. There is a car-ferry to Labuan. Inter-urban transport is provided by mini-buses, ordinary buses and taxis. Rates are reasonable. Air-conditioned, self-drive cars may be rented in Kota Kinabalu.

KOTA KINABALU

Charming, easy-going and attractive, Kota Kinabalu was largely destroyed during World War II, and has been rebuilt on reclaimed coast land on the South China Sea. Civic pride is evident in its clean, tree-lined streets. Locals speak good English and wear welcoming smiles. Getting around is easy – you can cover Kota Kinabalu on foot in 30 minutes. Sea breezes keep the temperature cooler than the oppressive heat of Kuala Lumpur. Shared taxis or mini-buses are best for local sightseeing. Kota Kinabalu is an excellent base. Allow two to three days here at the beginning or end of a visit to Sabah.

City Tour

A guided tour of Kota Kinabalu takes you past new department stores to the **State Mosque**. Further west, shaded by casuarina trees, is the **Tanjung Aru Beach** recreation centre with the Tanjung Aru Beach Hotel, the Golf Club and the Yacht Club. To the north is Likas Bay where the 30-storey glass tower of the Sabah Building soars skywards. Another interesting design is that of **Sabah Museum**, whose architecture incorporates Islam (the spires) and local culture in the outstretched arms of Dusun dancers (the eaves). Exhibits include ceramics, natural history and archive material on Sabah. In the garden is an excellent display of life-size tribal longhouses.
Open: daily 10.00–18.00 hrs, except Fridays. Admission free.

Accommodation

Kota Kinabalu lacks hotels to support large-scale tourism. Investment is planned for the Tanjung Aru beach area. **Borneo Resthouse**, PO Box 14799 (tel: (088) 718855). Comfortable 49-room hotel,

three miles (5km) from Kota
Kinabalu. Shuttle bus service.
Children's playground, baby-
sitters available. International
direct dialling, air-conditioning.
Cheap.

Hyatt Kinabalu International,
Jalan Datuk Salleh Sulong (tel:
(088) 221234). Comfortable
345-room hotel in central Kota
Kinabalu. When booking ask for
a room overlooking the South
China Sea. Streetside can be
noisy. First class facilities
include boutique, florist, pastry
shop and a business centre.
Large outdoor pool. A popular
hotel, very suitable for business
visitors. Expensive.

Palace Hotel, 1 Jalan Tangki,
Karamunsing, PO Box 10453 (tel:
(088) 211911). Moorish-style
hotel on a cool hillside within
walking distance of the large

Karamunsing Centre with shops
and restaurants. 160 air-
conditioned rooms, international
direct dialling, TV. Small
swimming-pool and gym. Nice
atmosphere and pleasant staff.
Cheap.

Sea View Hotel, PO Box 12004,
31 Jalan Haji Saman (tel: (088)
54422). 24 rooms. Small out-of-
town hotel near swimming
beaches. Good for young
travellers. Cheap.

Shangri-La Hotel, 75 Bandaran
Berjaya (tel: (088) 212800). 126
air-conditioned rooms in central
Kota Kinabalu. Comfortable with
a range of facilities. Visitors note
this is not a Shangri-La
International Hotel. Moderate.

Tanjung Aru Beach Hotel,
Locked Bag 174 (tel: (088)
58711). De luxe hotel managed
by Shangri-La International. 245

rooms and suites with balconies and sea or garden views. The most expensive rooms have individual jacuzzis, international direct dialling, TV and well-stocked mini-bar. Swimming-pool with jacuzzi, gym and sauna, four floodlit tennis courts, nautical sports centre and shops. Six miles (10km) from an 18-hole golf course. Around 15 minutes to Sabah Airport. Courtesy bus to town – 10 minutes walk. Taxis available. Expensive.

Food and Drink

Tourist hotels have Western and Asian menus. In Tanjung Aru, the **Garden Restaurant** serves good seafood (with a cultural show on Wednesdays and Saturdays). The **Golf View** (tel: 239151), serving Chinese dishes and live seafood, is popular but expensive. There are several moderately priced Chinese eating-places near the Hyatt. Hawker stalls are found along the harbour-front. The Tong Hing supermarkets sell delicious Chinese snacks and sandwiches, and also booze and soft drinks.

Nightlife

Kota Kinabalu has the only nightlife in Sabah. There are around 30 karaoke lounges and discos in leading hotels. People dress less formally than in Kuala Lumpur. Popular nightspots are **Tiffiny's** (sic), **Heart Beat** and the **Sandego Night Club**. The **Tiong Room** is an air-conditioned lounge with live music in the Tanjung Aru Beach Hotel (open 17.00–02.00 hrs). One of the best spots for a fun night out is the **Lazer Lounge** in the Palace Hotel – live music and karaoke.

Shopping

Shopping in Kota Kinabalu is excellent. **Yaoshan** and **Centrepoint** shopping complexes sell everything from Christian Dior fashions to gym-boots. You can buy cheap, attractive jewellery, pearls, baskets or macramé-work in the **Filipino Market**. A **Pasar Malam** (night market) sells cigarettes, cassettes, T-shirts. You must bargain in street markets. The **Sabah Handicraft Centre** is the place to look for local crafts.

Sabah Museum combines old and new

WHAT TO SEE IN SABAH

◆◆
GOMANTONG CAVES
20 miles (32km) south of Sandakan
The caves are a boat-ride across the bay from Sandakan (see page 77), followed by a 10-mile (16km) Landrover journey on jungle tracks. The caves are home for more than a million swifts which build nests among the roof-top stalactites. Twice yearly, men perform death-defying ascents 300 feet (90m) up flimsy bamboo ladders to collect the nests. A famous Chinese delicacy, they fetch big money abroad. Visits arranged by **SI Tours** in Sandakan.

◆◆◆
KINABALU NATIONAL PARK/ GUNUNG KINABALU
about 60 miles (100km) from Kota Kinabalu
Gunung Kinabalu reaches 13,455 feet (4,101m) and is known by the Dusun people as 'Akinabalu' – 'home of departed spirits'. The ascent begins from Kinabalu National Park, 296 square miles (767sq km) of lush tropical forest covering the mountain slopes. About 15 minutes outside Kota Kinabalu, turn right at the junction for Kinabalu. It is a two-hour drive up to the park. Along the way tribal people work in fields overhung with smoke from slash-and-burn cultivation. The entrance to Kinabalu Park is indicated; the office to register for climbing Gunung Kinabalu is on your right. A map shows local trails. The park is a paradise for naturalists as well as mountaineers. Behind the Park Headquarters are well laid out paths, and a charming mountain garden contains species such as *Nepenthes rajah*, or pitcher plants, which flourish at higher altitudes. Over 1,200 species of orchids are among the park exotica. There is hostel and chalet-type accommodation available, with cooking facilities – bookings through The Director, Sabah Parks Office, Kota Kinabalu. A twice-daily local bus service runs between Kota Kinabalu and Ranau, the nearest town to Gunung Kinabalu. Travelling time to the Park Headquarters is two hours. Take what you need for an overnight stay, as there is scarcely time to return by bus on the same day. Comfortable walking shoes and a warm, waterproof jacket are advisable.

Climbing Gunung Kinabalu
The ascent of Gunung Kinabalu is an unforgettable experience, but do not attempt the climb without preparation. You will hear that it is relatively easy for anyone fit, but this is not necessarily true. The ascent is steep and your knees feel it. Smokers in particular will have respiration problems in the thin air, and headaches, giddiness and nausea are commonly experienced. The best advice, is to follow one month's training before leaving home. Concentrate on building up your leg muscles. Even so, you will suffer muscle fatigue on this two-day trip.
First-time climbers may find the following advice useful:
● Do not carry anything in your hands. Use a light waterproof backpack.

Plan carefully to climb Kinabalu

- Pack what you want the porters to carry inside a durable plastic bag.
- On the first day pack your lunch to eat *en route*. Sandwiches and chocolate bars are recommended. Carry a plastic mineral water bottle.
- It is very important not to feel you have to keep the pace set by the guide. Find your own comfortable pace and keep this rhythm.
- On Day 1 wear loose shorts/light clothing.
- On Day 2 you need warm clothes – the final climb is done in sub-zero temperatures. Take a thermal vest, thick sweater and waterproof jacket, preferably with a hood. A woollen balaclava and gloves are essential. Wear tough rock-climbing boots and pack at least three extra pairs of socks.
- Other essentials are a torch, toilet items, especially sunscreen lotion and lip-salve, sweets, nuts and packet drinks. On Day 2 breakfast is at dawn and your next meal will not be until you return to Laban Rata base-camp (around 10.00 hrs).

◆◆◆
KOTA KINABALU–TENOM TRAIN RIDE

This trip is recommended for train enthusiasts (a pity the engine is not steam). The 95-mile (154km) journey begins at Kota Kinabalu railway station/Tanjung Aru and passes through the small towns of Papar and Beaufort *en route* to Tenom. The most exciting part is the Beaufort-Tenom stretch, when the track follows the Padas river boiling through the Padas Gorge and rainforest runs down to the river bank. Elsewhere the scenery varies from coastal swampland to cultivated paddy-fields. You can spend a night in Tenom, a good base to visit local Murut settlements. A hospitable tribe dependent on shifting cultivation, Murut build spectacular longhouses.

Accommodation

Hotel Perkasa Tenom, PO Box 225, Tenom (tel: (087) 735811). 10 rooms situated on a hill overlooking the town. Cheap.

◆◆◆
KUNDASSANG
about 40 minutes' drive from Kinabalu National Park
This small market-town at the foot of Mount Kinabalu is 45 minutes' drive from the picturesque Ranau Valley and Poring Hot Springs (see page 77). Local villagers are Dusun, farming and raising buffaloes.

Accommodation
Hotel Perkasa Mount Kinabalu, WDT II, Kundassang, Ranau (tel: (088) 889511 – booking office). Superbly situated 5,000 feet (1,500m) above sea-level, on a hilltop opposite Gunung Kinabalu. There are 74 comfortable rooms with TV. Efficiently run with friendly staff. Shop, games room with slot machines, karaoke lounge-bar and restaurant serving Western, Chinese and Malay meals. Airport pick-up from Kota Kinabalu by arrangement. Climbing preparations through the hotel. Nearby golf course. Rates are cheaper on weekdays. Moderate.

◆
MENGKABONG WATER VILLAGE
about 45 miles (72km) from Kota Kinabalu
This is an over-rated attraction. Most water-villages in Sabah are inhabited by former sea-gypsies/Filipino refugees. As their numbers grow, so these settlements extend further out to sea. Houses are interconnected by planks – watch your footing.

If you're feeling adventurous go for a wet and wild rafting trip down the Padas river

◆◆◆
PADAS RIVER
One of the most exhilarating excursions in Malaysia combines part of the train-ride to Tenom (see page 75) with rafting down the Padas river gorge. The day-tour is organised by **Borneo Expeditions** in Kota Kinabalu, who provide transfers, guides, equipment and lunch. After a 75-minute drive to Beaufort railway station, the train trip to the rafting site winds along the rocky Padas river gorge. You change into swimwear in the local station (basic WC), and basic safety instructions are given before you set out in the rubber raft. Life-jackets and crash-helmets are provided. Take nothing surplus on board as the raft may capsize. Cameras, change of clothes, etc, should be packed in a plastic box for transport back to the last part of the train journey. No one keeps dry on the Padas, a fast river with half a dozen tricky rapids. The 5½-mile (9km) ride takes around two hours.

◆◆◆
PORING HOT SPRINGS

near Ranau, 26 miles (43km)
from Kinabalu National Park
The springs are about two
hours' winding uphill drive. Few
experiences in Malaysia match
the luxury of lying in a private
tub in the heart of the jungle.
Open: daily, from 06.30 hrs to
sunset.

A **Wild Orchid Garden** is
located about 10 minutes' walk
behind the football pitch. The
Canopy Tree Walk is highly
recommended although
unsuitable for vertigo sufferers.
The walkway runs above the
tree-tops for half a mile (1km) –
a world of birds, squirrels and
flying foxes, guaranteed
unforgettable.
Open: 09.00–16.00 hrs. Pay at the
entrance to the springs (extra
for a camera and video-camera).

Accommodation

Chalet-type accommodation is
available. Also a youth hostel
(Poring Hostel, tel: (088) 218620).
Very cheap. Local store, but
bring supplies and drinks.

◆
SANDAKAN

on the Sulu Sea 240 miles
(386km) from Kota Kinabalu
The main reason for going to
Sandakan is to visit the **Sepilok
Orang-Utan Sanctuary** (see
page 79). MAS operates three
flights a day to Sandakan which
provide excellent views of
Gunung Kinabalu. The former
capital of North Borneo,
Sandakan was founded on
spices and gun-smuggling. A
timber boom town in the 1970s,
it is a busy commercial port of
minor tourist interest.
Near the 18-hole golf course on
the airport road is the **Forest
Research Centre**. The Exhibition
Centre features models of
logging camps, traditional
timbering methods, wood types
and habitats and crafts made
from woods. Photography is not
allowed. Of special interest is a
Rafflesia arnoldii specimen in
the reception centre. It is your
only chance of seeing this giant
parasitic flower, growing only in
specific mountain areas in
Sabah.
Open: 08.00–14.15 hrs from
Monday to Friday and 08.00–
12.45 hrs Saturday. Closed
Sunday.
Back in town, the market is
worth a visit and there is a
water village, but little else to
warrant spending more than a
couple of hours. Note that
Sandakan is very hot and there
is nowhere to swim except at a
small public pool. Avoid this
coast of Sabah during the
monsoon season June to August
and October to late February.
Special Interest Tours from
Sandakan are organised by SI

Tours, Lot 106, 1st Floor, Lai Ping Kee Building, 90008 Sandakan (tel: (089) 219717). They include jungle treks, butterfly collecting, camping and boating on the Kinabatangaan river. There are also day trips to Gomantong Caves (nest collection times January to February – see page 74). Airport transfers.

Accommodation
Hotel City View, Lot 1, Block 23, 3rd Avenue (tel: (089) 271122). A small, pleasant, air-conditioned hotel located in the heart of Sandakan. Rooms have international direct dialling, TV and mini-bar. Ground floor restaurant serves Western meals. English-style bacon and eggs, etc for breakfast. Moderate.

Ramada Renaissance Hotel, KMI, Jalan Utara (tel: (089) 213299). About 15 minutes' walk from Sandakan, the 120-room, air-conditioned hotel integrates the old Sabah Hotel with the 1911 Governor's House. Comfortable rooms with international direct dialling, TV, mini-bar and desk. Tennis, squash, work-out equipment and swimming-pool available; also business centre and disco. Bookings are essential in this retreat from the heat. Recommended. Expensive.

Restaurants
Western fare is available in the above hotels. There are cheap Muslim restaurants on Jalan Praya – the street on the waterfront. Very cheap Chinese hawker-style meals are sold above the Central Market.

◆◆◆
SEMPORNA AND PULAU SIPADAN
Semporna is an interesting old port town on the Celebes Sea. Access is by MAS flight from Kota Kinabalu to Tawau followed by a two-hour road-trip. Part of Semporna's charm is that it is totally off the tourist track. The **Dragon Inn** offers basic accommodation, built on stilts in the harbour. Local eating-places serve Chinese and seafood meals. Most visitors are divers, bound for the island of Sipadan – 22 miles (36km) offshore. Experienced divers rate it among the best sites in the world. Visibility is around 65 feet (20m) and the coral gardens teem with reef fish. Barracuda, sharks and turtles (especially between August and December) are common. The island has beautiful white-sand beaches.
Birdwatchers can observe frigatebirds, sea eagles and terns. Migratory species such as Nicobar pigeon are visitors during the colder months. Robber crabs scuttle about at night. Life on Sipadan is simple. A-frame beach-huts provide accommodation for 30, sharing. There are two male and two female ablutions facilities. Buffet-style meals are served in one large open hut – generous portions of mainly Chinese-Malay style seafood, including lobster. It is essential to bring everything you are likely to require – especially sunscreen lotion and reading material. Highly recommended. Packaged by **Borneo Divers** in Kota Kinabalu.

◆◆◆
SEPILOK FOREST RESERVE AND ORANG-UTAN SANCTUARY

7 miles (11km) from Sandakan Airport

The reserve covers 10,000 acres (4,000 hectares) of virgin rainforest of paramount interest to scientists and nature-lovers. Almost 40 per cent of the best known hardwoods are found in the reserve, also climbers, palms, pandanus and mangrove swamp habitat. The reserve is rich in wildlife – orang-utan, proboscis monkey, gibbon, long-tailed macaque, barking deer, mouse deer, bearded pig, Malaysian sun-bear and pangolin are a few of the more dramatic species. Also recorded in Sepilok are 217 species of birds. The main interest is the orang-utan sanctuary, a rehabilitation centre for illegally captured animals, founded in 1964. Most are young orang-utans either confiscated, or brought in from logging camps. The little apes are slowly reconditioned to living in the wild again. You can watch them being fed on a platform in the jungle, 10 minutes' easy walk from the Nature Centre. Feeding time is 09.30–10.00 hrs.

Sepilok Nature Education Centre is open daily all year from 09.00 hrs. Admission free. Facilities include research library and audio-visual presentations for groups. Interested parties must book two weeks in advance. Soft drinks and WC are available in the reserve.

Independent travellers can

Orang-utans rescued from captivity are later released back into the wild, from the Sepilok Sanctuary

catch a bus marked 'Sepilok Batu 14' outside Sandakan Bus Station at the west end of the market. The service is unreliable and most tourists share a taxi, or take an organised day-return air tour on MAS from Kota Kinabalu. Catch the 07.30 flight and return on the 15.15. For overnight accommodation see **Sandakan** pages 77–8.

◆◆
TAWAU

southeast Sabah

The town lies on a good stretch of coast. It is easily accessible by MAS from Kota Kinabalu (flight time 40 minutes). Tawau has an attractive mosque. In the heart of town is a memorial to Allied forces, and there is also a Japanese war memorial. A half-day visit to a local Iban longhouse can be made by shared taxi.

Accommodation
Marco Polo Hotel, Jalan Clinic, PO Box 1003 (tel: (089) 777988). 150 rooms. Five minutes' drive from Tawau Airport. Rooms have international direct dialling, TV, in-house video movies. Booking advised.

◆◆◆
TUNKU ABDUL RAHMAN NATIONAL PARK
Five islands off Kota Kinabalu make up the Tunku Abdul Rahman National Park. The clear water and good coral reefs offer excellent swimming and diving. Most coral is accessible from the beach – good for anyone without snorkelling experience. Bring your own gear. You can make a tour of the five islands, or catch an island boat. Deserted on weekdays, the islands are busy at weekends. Fishing is not allowed.

Pulau Gaya Good diving, with the best sites off the northern beaches. There are simple shelters at Police Beach. Take everything you are likely to require.

Pulau Mamutik A rocky island, Mamutik has a fresh water well and basic shelters; camping permitted. Crowded at weekends and holidays.

Pulau Manukan This super get-away spot has comfortable chalet-type accommodation with simple cooking facilities (bring supplies from Kota Kinabalu), and restaurant. There is sheltered swimming and diving. Bookings are through: The Director, Sabah Parks Head Office, Lot 3, Block X, Sinsuran Complex, PO Box 10626.

Pulau Sapi Sapi is ideal for a family half-day trip. There are shelters, barbecue, showers and WC, and sand beaches with shady trees. The coral is easily accessible for non-experienced snorkellers.

Pulau Sulug Good snorkelling off the south end of the island, which is underdeveloped and very private. Camping is allowed with permission from the National Parks office in Kota Kinabalu. Do not forget insect repellent.

◆◆
TURTLE ISLANDS
This group of islands off Sandakan is worth visiting if turtles are your interest. The main breeding place, **Selingan Island**, has a hatchery. August to November is the best turtle-watching season, when green and hawksbill turtles come ashore to lay eggs. The boat-trip from Sandakan to Selingan takes 2½ to 3 hours. Basic rest-houses with cooking facilities are available, but bring food and drink from Sandakan. Fresh water is available. After dinner you can watch the turtles coming ashore – remember to bring a torch. The return trip is made early the next day. Fishing boats to the Turtle Islands are cheap, but unreliable. You are advised to charter a private boat, or to take a local tour.

STATE OF SARAWAK

In northwest Borneo, Sarawak shares common borders with Brunei, Sabah and Kalimantan. It has a steamy, equatorial climate with an average temperature of 32°C (90°F). The best time to visit is April to July. Sarawak's interest lies in its tribal cultures. There are 23 ethnic groups whose lifestyles remain

Skulls ward off evil spirits

essentially unchanged except that they are no longer headhunters. MAS operates daily air links between Kuala Lumpur and Kuching, Sarawak's capital. Royal Brunei Airlines and Merpati/Indonesian Airlines also link Brunei and Kalimantan. There is a domestic service to all the main towns in Sarawak from Kuching. Fares are economical. A surfaced road links Kuching in the south to Miri in the north. Elsewhere four-wheel drive may be necessary. River transport is important. An express boat service connects Kuching with other Sarawak towns. Travellers can use this means of transport along the coast, or to visit the hinterland. It is a thrilling way of sightseeing, accompanied by locals and all their belongings. Sarawak is rich in oil, gas, rubber and timber. It is the third largest producer of black pepper in the world.

KUCHING

Kuching is an atmospheric riverine town, 20 miles (32km) upstream from the South China Sea. Its busy waterfront bazaars are thronged with Chinese, Malays and local tribesmen. The town rises from coastal swamps to hills. The second Rajah Brooke selected the main hill to build his palace, or **Istana**. Kuching consists of two districts: the waterfront bazaars and the Padungan area, site of recent commercial growth. To enjoy the atmosphere, walk along the river which bustles with small craft loading and unloading goods from the

Boatmen on the serene river waters near Kuching

hinterland – copra, sago, coconuts and fruits. At dusk hire a boat for an hour's cruise before sunset (bargain the cost). A city tour (duration three hours) is recommended to see the main highlights such as the **State Mosque**, the **Law Courts** and **Sarawak Museum**. *Enquiries:* **C P H Travel Agencies:** 70 Padungan Road, 93714 Kuching (tel: (082) 243708). There is a branch in the Sarawak Plaza.

WHAT TO SEE

◆◆
COURT HOUSE

This symbol of colonial power on the riverfront was erected by the Second Rajah, Charles Brooke, in 1874. The clock tower was added in 1883. A monument to the Second Rajah stands in front.

◆◆
FORT MARGHERITA

Situated downstream from the Istana, the fort is named after the wife of the Second Rajah. Built in 1878, it was used to defend Kuching from attacks by sea pirates. Access to the fort, now a Police Museum, is by small ferry or *tambang*.

◆◆
GENERAL POST OFFICE

In central Kuching, this is an imposing building from the 1930s, with a Corinthian-type façade.

◆◆
ISTANA

The palace, built in 1870 by Rajah Charles Brooke, exudes images from the colonial era. It sits among rolling lawns on the north bank of the Sarawak river; the best views of it are from the bank opposite. The palace is now the official residence of Sarawak's head of state, and is not open to visitors.

◆◆
MASJID BESAR (STATE MOSQUE)

In central Kuching, the mosque is an imposing monument to Islam. Built in 1968, it stands on the site of an earlier wooden mosque. Visitors may enter if they are suitably dressed.

◆
PAVILION

Situated opposite the General Post Office, this is one of Kuching's oldest buildings. The colonial-style Pavilion now houses Government offices.

◆◆◆
SARAWAK MUSEUM

The museum is a treasure-trove for the visitor interested in local archaeology and culture. Originally opened in 1891, it depicts the history and ethnological background of Sarawak's many indigenous tribes. Exhibits include a diorama on the Stone Age excavations from the Niah Caves, early tools and weapons, also weaving. Several rooms are devoted to the fauna of North Borneo. Do not miss the Kajaman burial-pole in the garden. A landscaped park opposite the museum has a café serving refreshments.
Open: daily 10.00–18.00 hrs, except Fridays. Admission free.

◆◆
SQUARE TOWER

This example of tropical nostalgia for Renaissance England was originally a detention centre. During the Brooke era, it doubled as a fortress and dance-hall.

◆◆
TUA PEK KONG TEMPLE

On Jalan Tunku Abdul Rahman, the temple is around a century old. It is famous for its Wang Kang celebration to commemorate the spirits of the dead.

Accommodation

Kuching counts some 50 hotels, but there is a lack of tourist-style facilities. Up-country towns offer reasonable, moderately priced accommodation.

Borneo Hotel, 30-C-F Jalan Tabuan (tel: (082) 244121). Comfortable with 44 rooms. Moderate to cheap.

Holiday Inn Kuching, PO Box 2363, Jalan Tunku Abdul Rahman (tel: (082) 423111). Near the river and central commercial area, it has 320 rooms with first class facilities. International direct dialling, TV, mini-bar, pool. Moderate to expensive.

Kuching Hilton, PO Box 2396, Jalan Tunku Abdul Rahman (tel: (082) 248200/1). Near the river and Sarawak Mall, it has 322 air-conditioned rooms all with international direct dialling, TV and mini-bar. Malay/Chinese/Western cuisine. Moderate to expensive.

Mayfair Hotel, 45-47 Jalan Palm (tel: (082) 421486). About five minutes' taxi-ride from the Sarawak river, it has 42 rooms. Cheap.

Nightlife

Entertainment in Sarawak is relatively low-key. Leading hotels usually have live music with a female singer. The Hilton and Holiday Inn have a bar-disco.

Restaurants

Market stalls sell a variety of local delicacies. You can also eat cheaply in open-air restaurants such as **Batu Lintang** on Market Street, **Kubah Ria** (at Petra Jaya) and **Bukit Mata Kuching Food Centre**. Tastes range from delicate to highly spiced. Up-market dining in Kuching can be had at the **Serapi Restaurant** in the Holiday Inn and the **Kuching Hilton Restaurant** – Malay/Chinese/Western. **New Jakarta** restaurant serves Malay/Indonesian food at moderate cost. **Lok Thian** restaurant, two miles (3km) from the centre of Kuching, enjoys a good reputation for Chinese and Thai food.

Shopping

Sarawak is known for a vast array of traditional handicrafts. Each ethnic group has a unique style of craftsmanship, producing vibrant patterns in a multitude of colours. Good buys are hand-woven Iban cloth, Melanau Terindek hats, Penan sleeping mats, Bidayah tambok baskets, jewellery and curios. The best place to browse in Kuching is the **Main Bazaar**, Wayang and Temple Streets. The colourful **Sunday Open Market** on Jalan Satok is highly recommended. Occasionally a superb tribal antique turns up among the fruit and vegetables. Recommended souvenir shops: **Borneo Handicraft Shop**, 6 Jalan

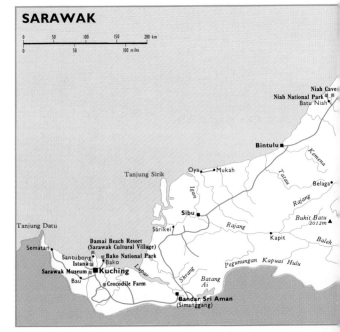

Traditional Dyak longhouses

Tun Abg Hj Openg; **Chung Nan Trading**, 14 Lebuh Khoo Hun Yeang; **Eeze Trading**, Lot 289 Ground Floor, Jalan Ban Hock (also Kuching International Airport). **Sarawak Art Shop**, Museum New Wing, sells wood carvings, baskets, Iban blankets, parangs or machetes, bead necklaces and other tribal jewellery. Indigenous motifs are also found on local pottery. Do not miss a visit to the pottery factory Batu 5, Jalan Penrissen. Several other pottery factories are found along the Old Airport Road in Kuching. Kuching boasts several air-conditioned shopping complexes for general and Western-type goods – **Wisma Saberkas, Sarawak Plaza, Wisma Phoenix** and **Kuching Plaza** on the main street, Jalan McDougall, sell everything you may need.

WHAT TO SEE IN SARAWAK

◆◆◆
CROCODILE FARM
18 miles (29km) from Kuching
This is a popular stop-over for tourists making the Skrang river trip (see page 88). Around a thousand crocodiles are bred here for skin and meat. You can see saltwater and freshwater crocodiles. Other animals to be seen are monkeys, squirrels, sun bears and mongooses.
Open: daily.

◆◆◆
DAMAI BEACH RESORT
about 20 miles (32km) from Kuching
Near Santubong fishing village, the resort has a good swimming beach below Mount Santubong. Worth seeing is the Sarawak Cultural Village, built in natural rainforest on the mountain slopes. You can see exhibits of art and handicrafts, dances and demonstrations of the different ethnic cultures in Sarawak.

Accommodation
Holiday Inn Damai Beach Resort, PO Box 2870, 93756 Kuching (tel: (082) 411777). 202 rooms and chalets in a quiet, beachfront location. Swimming-pool with swim-up bar; tennis courts, squash and badminton; watersports. Diving equipment can be rented at the watersports centre. The best base for a stay of several days after sightseeing in Sarawak.

◆◆
GUNUNG MULU NATIONAL PARK
northwest Sarawak
The park contains 130,630 acres (52,866 hectares) of rainforest with a huge variety of plants, birds (including eight types of hornbill) and butterflies. There are three great caves within the park which are open to the public: **Deer Cave, Clearwater Cave** and **Wind Cave**. The Deer Cave has the largest passage in the world. The limestone pinnacles make dramatic photographs, but they are on the summit of a high limestone ridge. Climbing experience is necessary. Wear comfortable shoes, loose trousers and waterproof jacket. Take a torch and mosquito repellent. Basic accommodation sleeps 20 persons overnight. (See **Peace and Quiet**, page 95).

◆◆◆
IBAN LONGHOUSE VISIT
Curiosity about tribal culture attracts many tourists to Sarawak. Iban, who comprise 30 per cent of the state's population, live communal lifestyles in a longhouse. This is exactly as the name implies: it is a very long house – some may have as many as 100 rooms shared by 50 families all living under the same roof. Longhouses are raised on stilts about three feet (1m) above the ground. To enter you climb up a ladder, or a notched log. Family rooms open off a central hall, whose cane floor creaks as you walk on it. Eating and socialising take place in the hall, or *ruai*. Chores such as pounding rice and weaving baskets are done on the veranda. Dogs, pigs and ducks forage beneath for food. The handsome red-and-orange plumed cocks are used in cock

fights, a popular leisure-time activity. Not so very long ago the Ibans were head-hunters. Today they plant a few crops and entertain visitors. Men decorate their backs and thighs with blue tattooed flower and bird motifs. Some wear tattoos around their throats like a collar. Women are bare-breasted. Visitors are traditionally offered sour rice wine from a communal vessel. Dismiss an urge not to drink it as this will cause offence.

Longhouses have no facilities and getting there means a hot walk through the jungle. Dress comfortably and do not forget your neck towel to wipe up perspiration. Some longhouses lie within a half-day's drive of Kuching. The Skrang river safari includes a longhouse visit (see page 88).

A safari from Kuching down the Skrang river will take you to the water village of the Sea Dyaks

MIRI
northwest Sarawak

Miri owes its existence to the discovery of oil – the first well in Malaysia – in 1910. The town lies 15 miles (25km) down the coast from the mouth of the Baram river. Local swimming can be dangerous, but a scenic beach in the district is Brighton Beach. Miri is the jumping-off point for Niah Caves.

Accommodation

Miri has half a dozen moderately priced hotels which are used mainly by oil company employees and government visitors. Most offer comfortable, no-frills style facilities.

Apollo Hotel, 4 Jalan South Yu Seng (tel: (085) 33077). 19 rooms.

Gloria Hotel, PO Box 1283, 27 Jalan Brooke (tel: (085) 416699). 42 rooms.

Park Hotel Kingsway, Kingsway, PO Box 241, Miri (tel: (085) 414555). 95 rooms.

◆◆◆
NIAH CAVES
about 60 miles (100km) south of Miri

The caves lie in the Niah National Park (see **Peace and Quiet**, page 94). They are the major attraction in the 7,660-acre (3,103-hectare) park -- the Great Cave alone covers an area the size of 13 soccer fields. The caves caused a stir in anthropological circles in the 1950s when a human skull was discovered, estimated to be about 40,000 years old. Other finds indicated the Niahians lived in the caves from 40,000BC right up to AD1400. Cave drawings show the tribe had a unique culture and beliefs. In the 1400s they mysteriously disappeared although some ethnologists link them to the Penan – one of 23 Orang Asli (native peoples) living in Sarawak. The Penans collect edible birds' nests from the roof of the caves.

Getting There: There is a daily MAS flight Kuching–Miri. From Miri, the journey by road takes two hours. At Batu Niah you catch the park longboat, a 30-minute journey. The way to the Great Cave involves a 2½-mile (4km) walk along a raised wooden bridge which takes about 45 minutes (in wet weather it is slippery). Wear gym-boots and remember your torch.

Arrangements must be made in advance through the National Parks Office, Forest Development, Miri, Sarawak (independent travellers). Package tours stay overnight at the Park Hotel in Miri.

◆◆◆
SANTUBONG
20 miles (32km) from Kuching

This attractive fishing village has nearby swimming beaches. Siar Beach is a scenic spot with curious rock formations and unpolluted bays. Semantan Beach, a beautiful white sand beach, is two hours' drive from Siar. Popular at weekends.

◆◆
SIBU

The second town of Sarawak is reached by air and road from Kuching. The town's population of 30,000 includes many Chinese, mainly Foochow traders. Government offices, markets, churches, wharves and go-downs (warehouses) lie on a small, flat island in the Rejang river delta. Recent growth has been rapid. There are half a dozen comfortable, moderately priced hotels.

◆◆◆
SKRANG RIVER SAFARI

The trip is five hours by road and river from Kuching. About 43 miles (70km) before the Skrang river, the road winds into the Pegunungan Kapuas Hulu (Kapuas Mountains). Deep gorges, ravines overhung with rainforest and trees covered in wild orchids are seen. At the river jetty, a boat takes you to the longhouse of the Sea Dyaks. Visitors stay in a basic guest-house after a memorable night feasting and dancing with the Dyaks. Take mosquito repellent as well as overnight attire.

Organised by **Sarawak Travel** and other operators in Kuching. Highly recommended.

PEACE AND QUIET

Wildlife and Countryside in Malaysia
by Paul Sterry

Visitors to Malaysia cannot fail to be struck by its beauty and by the richness of its natural resources. Plant life burgeons in the tropical climate and an incredible diversity of trees and shrubs proliferates. Animal life is no less rich: everything from rhinos to slow lorises, hornbills to fruit bats is here somewhere. Away from the coastal fringe of sandy beaches and mangroves, this is the realm of tropical rainforest, and it is here that the main diversity of Malaysia's plant and animal life lies. A walk among the forest trees is an unforgettable experience, with birds and gibbons calling high above in the canopy and insect life teeming at your feet.

Malaysia's climate is truly tropical. Although temperatures vary little throughout the year, there is, however, considerable variation in the rainfall, due mainly to the fact that Peninsular Malaysia in particular is surrounded on all sides by the sea. There is no true 'dry' season but there are seasons of high and low rainfall. These vary throughout Malaysia as a whole according to the direction of the prevailing monsoon wind. Visitors would do well to anticipate the rainfall to be expected because, for example, many parts of the coast are impossible to visit during the rainy season. There are two types of monsoon winds that affect Malaysia. The northeast monsoon brings rain

Trees can soar to great heights

from October to March and affects mainly eastern Peninsular Malaysia and Sabah and Sarawak. The southwest monsoon brings rain from April to August and affects mainly western Peninsular Malaysia. It is the coastal areas that are affected most by the rainfall: visitors should plan this part of their trip carefully. Inland areas at higher elevation are generally influenced to a much lesser degree by the extremes of rainfall.

Tropical Rainforests

Mangrove forests flourish around the coast, while in areas of freshwater, swamp forest predominates. However, on *terra firma* it is tropical rainforest that is the natural vegetation. At one time these forests would have blanketed much of Malaysia. Although a considerable amount has been felled, there are still wonderful areas of rainforest left and many of these lie within the protective boundaries of national parks and reserves.

Many of the trees in the rainforests reach huge proportions. They may stand over 150 feet (50m) in height, their huge trunks being supported at the base by buttress roots which spread out over the thin soils. The diversity of the trees is also astonishing. It is most unusual to find two of the same species growing side by side: within an area of just a few acres of virgin rainforest there might be several hundred species.

Rainforests support an amazing range of animal life, although the creatures are often difficult to locate. For example, many birds and monkeys haunt the tree canopy, but they are often well over 100 feet (30m) above the forest floor, so that tantalising glimpses are all you are likely to get unless you try a few simple tactics. One of these is to use any slope in the ground to your advantage: looking downhill will enable you to see the canopy of trees below without the effort of twisting your neck.

The Tualang Tree

The tualang is Malaysia's largest native tree, often towering above the surrounding forest. Strange as it may seem, this wonder is a member of the pea family. Wild bees often make their nests among the branches, which encourages local people not to fell it, since they are very fond of honey. The timber is also extremely hard and difficult to cut, so the tualang is under less threat than other rainforest trees.

Dense vegetation still survives

Mangroves

Although beautiful sandy beaches are a feature of many parts of the Malaysian coast, in some areas mangroves form the boundary between sea and land. Mangroves are trees whose root systems can tolerate both immersion in seawater for part of the day and exposure to air for the rest. They grow in thick sandy mud and are important agents in the creation and consolidation of new land. Mangrove root systems form a tangled network which allows silt and mud to settle. Not surprisingly, there is little oxygen found below the surface layers here, and to combat this, the mangroves produce aerial roots in addition to those responsible for anchoring the trees. Several different species of mangrove are found around the Malaysian coast, each with a slightly different tolerance to exposure to saltwater and air. Mangroves harbour a rich community of animals. Fiddler crabs dot the surface of the muddy channels and creeks and mudskippers – curious fish that seem as happy out of water as in it – are often abundant. The mangroves also act as nurseries for fish of the open water. With this abundance of life it is no wonder that herons, egrets, waders and kingfishers have little shortage of food.

Excursions from Kuala Lumpur

Those on a short visit to the capital and who want to experience something of Malaysia's natural riches, should visit the Batu Caves, seven miles (12km) north of Kuala Lumpur. The caves themselves are home to cave nectar bats, and long-tailed macaques frequent the surrounding forest. The turning to the caves is signposted off the Ipoh road. Another good destination is the small remnant of rainforest 14 miles (22km) north of Kuala Lumpur at Templer Park (Hutan Kanching), on the road to Rawang.

Ampang Forest Reserve

This is another excellent destination for visitors to Kuala Lumpur with only a short time to spend but who wish to explore an area of rainforest, since it is less than an hour's drive from Kuala Lumpur. The forest reserve protects the catchment area for a reservoir, which is the main reason why it has escaped being felled.
An early morning walk through the forest is best. Move quietly and slowly, listening for calls among the foliage and rustling sounds on the forest floor. Although not necessarily shy, many of the forest birds will remain motionless among the dappled leaves while visitors pass by. It is often a good idea to stand still for a few minutes just to see what emerges from cover.

Taman Negara

This was Malaysia's first national park – and it is perhaps the finest and most accessible area of unspoilt forest in the whole country. The Tembeling and Tahan rivers run through the park, flanked by immense trees covered in epiphytic plants. Birdlife abounds and some of

PEACE AND QUIET

the country's most threatened mammals are found here. The park is closed from mid-November until mid-January because of dangerous water levels, but for the rest of the year it can be reached by boat from Jerantut. This is reached by bus or taxi from Kuala Lumpur. Visitors would be well advised to book the boat and accommodation in advance with the Wildlife National Park Department in Kuala Lumpur. The park headquarters are at Kuala Tahan, where there is accommodation for about 200 people. From here numerous well-marked trails lead off into the forest, some of which can be undertaken in a day, others need several days. On some of the trails there are hides in which visitors can stay overnight. Information about all of the facilities can be obtained from the headquarters.

The Cameron Highlands

Discovered in 1885 by government surveyor William Cameron, this upland region of Peninsular Malaysia is a welcome retreat from the heat and humidity of the coast. Although level land is often cultivated – the Cameron Highlands is an important producer of tea and vegetables – many of the hill slopes still retain their natural vegetation. Here cloud forests predominate, with huge tree ferns being particularly characteristic of clearings and open areas.
The area is easy to reach either by car or by public transport. Drive north from Kuala Lumpur and at Tapah turn off on to the

upland road; buses also follow this route. Tanah Rata makes a good base from which to explore the area and there are numerous trails and paths to follow. One particularly good one leads to Gunung Beremban; information about this and other walks can be obtained from the information office in Tanah Rata.

Kuala Selangor Nature Park

This park lies near Kuala Selangor on the west coast of Peninsular Malaysia about 40 miles (65km) from Kuala Lumpur. In addition to natural coastal forests and mangroves, there are man-made lakes and specially built birdwatching hides here. An information centre at Bukit Melawati (open Saturdays) provides additional information about the area. Visitors can find waders, herons, kingfishers and other wetland birds among the mangrove swamps. Short-clawed otters are also frequently seen, but the highlights are the silvered leaf monkeys, which, thanks to protection, have become tame and approachable. This is one of the rarest monkeys in Malaysia and Kuala Selangor provides visitors with the best opportunities of seeing them in the wild.

The Langkawi Islands

The 99 Langkawi Islands lie off the northwest coast of Peninsular Malaysia. Largest of these is Langkawi, whose centre is Kuah; the town and indeed much of the island is dominated by the peak of Gunung Raya. To reach the main island, visitors can either

fly from Kuala Lumpur or catch
a ferry from Kuala Perlis. A
distinct dry season means that
the climate of this region is
rather different from most other
parts of Peninsular Malaysia.
Apart from the idyllic setting of
the islands, surrounded as they
are by the Indian Ocean, one of
their major attractions is their
comparatively undeveloped and
unspoilt nature. For although
there are rubber plantations and
agricultural plots on Langkawi,
dense patches of tropical forest
still cloak much of the land.
Long-tailed macaques are a
common sight, but also look for
dusky leaf monkeys, a small
species with conspicuous white
rings around the eyes.
Tranquil bays are a feature of
the coast and allow relaxation in
almost complete isolation if you
are prepared to travel; a good
road allows easy exploration of
Langkawi Island. Most of the
other islands are completely
unspoilt, and Pulau Dayang
Bunting (the 'island of the
pregnant girl') in particular
makes a wonderful trip.

Penang Island
On the outskirts of Georgetown,
the island's capital, are the
Penang Botanical Gardens
(catch bus 7 from the centre). In
addition to the gardens
themselves, the area is
surrounded by forested slopes
which are home to a variety of
wildlife, most noticeably the
troops of long-tailed macaques.
These animals are accustomed
to the presence of man and
indeed often demand feeding
with peanuts!
Near the fishing village of Pantai

Aceh on the northwest coast is
the Pantai Aceh Forest Reserve
which safeguards the best
remaining area of native
woodland. The turning to the
village is just south of the Titi
Kerawang Waterfall. There is
also a butterfly farm in the north
of the island near Teluk Bahang.
Penang Island can be reached
from the mainland via the
immense Penang Bridge from
Butterworth.

Fraser's Hill
This is a large area of forested
mountain ranges within which
lies the 7,360-acre (2,980-
hectare) Fraser's Hill Wildlife
Sanctuary. Bukit Fraser, the
area's principal town, lies 62 miles
(100km) north of Kuala Lumpur;
to reach it, drive north from the

A native pig-tailed monkey

PEACE AND QUIET

Malay fruit or common dog-faced bat

capital on the Ipoh road and turn off at Kuala Kubu Bahru. There are hotels and guesthouses in Bukit Fraser but visitors would be well advised to book accommodation in advance.

There are numerous trails and paths leading from Bukit Fraser; enquire where you are staying for details. The forests are spectacular, with huge tree farms and *dipterocarp* trees; birds of prey soar over the hill slopes, and there are monkeys in the tree canopy.

Bako National Park (Sarawak)

Established in 1957, Bako is the oldest national park in Sarawak and also the most accessible; it lies on a coastal peninsula in the west of Sarawak and is less than 25 miles (40km) from Kuching

(regular bus service). At the park headquarters in Teluk Assam there is an information centre with exhibits and maps and routes of the trails and paths which allow visitors to explore the area. Most of the trails can be walked in a day, although for some you will have to be prepared to camp. The park is closed between October and March (the rainy season) and for the rest of the year visitors are strongly advised to book accommodation in advance.

The park boasts a wide variety of habitats, from mangrove swamps and tropical forests to sandy beaches and freshwater pools and waterfalls. Proboscis monkeys can be seen around the mangroves, long-tailed macaques are ubiquitous and often indifferent to human presence, but flying lemurs are perhaps the most exciting of the park's animal residents. These intriguing mammals have membranous skin stretching between the front and hind legs and between the hind legs and the tail. The result is a continuous, aerodynamic sheet which allows the animal to glide from tree to tree.

Niah Caves (Sarawak)

The caves lie in the Niah and Lambir Hills National Parks on the hilly coast of northern Sarawak. They are well known for the extraordinary range of cave dwelling creatures found in the extensive system.

The cave system lies near Batu Niah, accessible either by bus or taxi from the town of Miri. The headquarters of the national park are at Pangkalan Lubang (accommodation also available); from here visitors can either walk or take a boat trip to the mouth of the caves. Many people choose to hire a guide. This is not only a useful means of getting the most from the caves but is obligatory if you wish to visit the Painted Cave. Within the caves, several million

Proboscis Monkey
The extraordinary proboscis monkey is found only on Borneo; visitors to Sarawak and Sabah stand a good chance of seeing this bizarre creature if the right locations are visited.
The most characteristic feature of this monkey, and the one after which it is named, is of course the strange, proboscis-like nose, which increases in size in the male as he ages. As his nose grows, he gradually acquires a harem of up to a dozen females, which he guards jealously. Proboscis monkeys live in mangrove swamps and riverine forests, often moving many miles inland from the coast. They feed on leaves and seeds and, because food is slow to digest, they have huge, swollen bellies. Males are particularly large and may weigh as much as 40 pounds (18kg). Despite their bulky appearance, they spend most of their lives in the trees and are agile and sure-footed when leaping from branch to branch. They are also quite willing and able to swim from one side of a river to the other. Proboscis monkeys are most easily seen at the Samansam Wildlife Sanctuary in Sarawak, for which prior permission is necessary for a visit. They also occur on the coastal reaches of the Kinabatangan River in Sabah and in the Bako National Park.

cave swiftlets nest, and bats roost. The swiftlets' nests are harvested by licence outside the breeding season to be used in bird's nest soup.

Gunung Mulu National Park (Sarawak)
Gunung Mulu, dominated by the 7,800-foot (2,377m) peak of the same name, lies close to the Brunei border in northwest Sarawak and comprises 130,960 acres (53,000 hectares) of forested hills as well as one of the most extensive cave systems in the world.
A permit must be obtained in advance from the Forestry Department Office in Miri to visit the park. From here, take a taxi or bus to Marudi and then a boat to the park headquarters. Trails of various lengths allow visitors to explore the hills and mountains as well as some of the more accessible caves.

Sepilok Forest Reserve (Sabah)
For most visitors to Sabah, the Sepilok Forest Reserve has become synonymous with the Orang-Utan Rehabilitation Centre. However, there is much more to see in the area; the unspoilt tropical forest harbours a wide variety of birds, and mangroves fringe the estuaries. To reach the reserve and centre, take a bus from Sandakan, 15 miles (24km) away. The rehabilitation centre was established to 'train' young orang-utan, illegally taken from the wild, to be able to lead a natural life in the wild again. There is a Nature Education Centre as well as paths and trails that lead through the forest

and these are ideal for birdwatching. One of them leads to a feeding platform where orang-utans that have partially returned to the wild come for food when called.

Gunung Kinabalu (Sabah)

At 13,455 feet (4,101m), Gunung Kinabalu is the highest peak in Southeast Asia. Much of the area surrounding the mountain has been designated a national park and is geared up to cope with visitors of a more adventurous and energetic nature. The park headquarters can be reached by bus from Kota Kinabalu, but your visit to the park must be registered in advance with the Sabah National Parks office in Kota Kinabalu.

There are trails and paths around the forest headquarters and information in the display centre. The whole area is a botanical treasure house: because of the altitudinal range within the park's boundaries, the numbers of flower species is vast and includes over 1,000 species of orchids and six species of rhododendrons.

> **Orang-utans**
> The name orang-utan literally means 'old man of the forest'. Having seen them at the rehabilitation centre at Sepilok, and seen how quickly they acquire human traits, this name seems particularly appropriate. Orang-utans have long arms and legs and their powerful grip – both feet and hands – enables them to be completely at ease among the branches of the forest trees. They even make their nests in the trees in which they spend the night; a new nest is made each evening.
> Despite strict legislature, orang-utans are still threatened by illegal capture from the wild, but their greatest threat now lies in the loss, or rather fragmentation of their habitat. They need large tracts of tropical forest in order to survive, and in order to maintain a viable long-term population there must be some mixing with groups from other areas. Felling of rainforest for its hardwood timber is the most pernicious and serious threat to the apes, as well as to all the other forest inhabitants.

Setting out in Kinabalu Park

FOOD AND DRINK

The variety of exotic foods
available in Malaysia is without
parallel in Southeast Asia.
Eating out is also very cheap.
The locals' love of food is
reflected in countless
restaurants, cafés, food-bars and
market stalls. You can dine in
the elegant surroundings of a
top hotel, or tuck in at an
open-air hawker stand. If you
don't know what to order, ask a
local. You are likely to be
invited to join his table. The
main ethnic groups – Malay,
Chinese and Indian – all
contribute to the bewildering
array of foods. All tourist hotels
feature Western menus, and
popular outlets like Kentucky
Fried and Dunkin' Doughnuts
are found in Kuala Lumpur and
Penang.

Malay cuisine resembles both
Indian and Indonesian cooking.
Most dishes are characterised
by the liberal addition of spices,
chillies and coconut cream.
Subtle differences in flavours
are found from state to state.
Pulau Pinang (Penang) and
Perak are reputed for their
gastronomy. *Satay* is a
traditional Malay dish: cubes of
skewered chicken and beef are
dipped in hot, peanut sauce
with side-serves of rice and
cucumber to cool your taste
buds. *Satay* is usually eaten as a
starter. A popular main course is
nasi padang (steamed rice
surrounded by dishes of curried
meat, chicken, seafood and
vegetables). The words *ikan*
and *ayam* appear on every
menu. *Ikan* (fish) is cooked in a
hundred different ways. *Ikan
panggang*, baked in banana
leaves and served with chilli
and dried shrimp paste sauce,
is very popular. Malays eat lots
of chicken *(ayam)* since their
religion forbids pork. *Ayam
panggang* is chicken pieces
marinaded in coconut cream
and herbs barbecued over
charcoal. *Ayam kapitan* is an
aromatic curry made from
chicken, chilli, lemon grass and
coconut cream. There are
endless soups to sup before or
during a meal (the Chinese
way). *Laksa asam* and *laksa
lemak* are both delicious. The
first is a sour rice noodle soup
based on fish stock; the second
is a coconut and noodle curry
sauce flavoured with prawns,
liver and other titbits. A Malay
breakfast is worth trying if you
like savoury tastes in the
morning. *Nasi dagang* is a
combination of rice with coconut
milk garnished with onions,
shallots, ginger and other
spices. It is especially popular
on the east coast. Tourist hotels
always have a choice of local
and Western dishes. Most hotel
coffee-bars serve snacks such
as pizza, hamburgers and
ice-cream. Malay desserts using
shaved ice may cause a
stomach upset. If you cannot
resist the temptation, try ABC
(ali batur campur) a chilled ice
mountain sweetened with palm
sugar, sweet corn, red beans
and jelly cubes. In most places
you can eat without fear.
Hawker stalls are rigorously
supervised by health inspectors.
Seafood is often still kicking.
Juices are made from freshly
harvested fruits before your
very eyes. (See **Fruits**, page 98.)

FOOD AND DRINK

Chinese restaurants outnumber places selling Malay food. In many towns you may search in vain for a Malay food-shop. Most Chinese dishes come from Cantonese and Hokkien kitchens. Menus are always long and confusing, but all feature soup, meat, seafood and vegetables. Now is your chance to try something really exotic like bird's nest soup or *yam pot* – dishes which cost a fortune in the West.

Malacca is the home of Nonya or Peranakan cooking devised by Straits-born Chinese. Nonya dishes are big on spices, chillies, lemon grass, *belacan* (prawn paste) and coconut cream. *Laksa* is a superb sweet-sour soup. Prawn and liver-ball soups are also Nonya. Other things to try are *otak-otak* (spicy fish cake) and *garam assam* (seafood). *Gula melaka* is a favourite sweet dessert based on sago topped with palm sugar and coconut milk. Nonya cooking extends south to Johor and Singapore. The northern states of Malaysia are heavily influenced by Thai cooking.

Locally grown tea and coffee are popular beverages in Malaysia. Some hotels provide facilities for making your own. Mini-bars contain a choice of imported alcoholic beverages. Local beer is excellent, but carbonated drinks are disappointing. Stick to well known mineral water brands such as Alpine, Mountain View, Pine – others may be made from tapwater. Fresh juices are sold everywhere. Large department stores sell chilled beverages – guava, water melon, mango – in sanitary conditions.

Fruits

Tropical fruits flourish in Malaysia. Some are now imported into Europe. Ask the trader to identify unfamiliar ones in the market.

Carambola, or starfruit, is a shiny, bright yellow fruit available year-round. Fresh starfruit juice is popular. The nutrients are said to be good for high blood pressure.

Cempadak is a large fruit the size of a football with dozens of seeds sunk in fragrant, yellow flesh. Street-traders fry sliced *cempadak* in batter like sweet potato.

Durian is a large, spiky fruit available in June–August and November–February. Its delicious, soft yellow flesh smells like overripe cheese. Several hotels forbid you to bring durian inside.

Guava is a fresh tasting fruit also drunk as a refreshing beverage. It is said to contain five times the amount of vitamin C in orange juice.

Mangosteen is a popular fruit which follows the durian season. Round and purple-skinned, its translucent white segments have a slightly tart taste similar to litchi.

Rambutan is a bright red, hairy fruit indigenous to Malaysia. You peel the skin off revealing white flesh around a single brown seed.

Pomelo, also called a shaddock, is a large member of the citrus fruit family. Pomelo are exchanged as gifts by the Chinese at New Year.

SHOPPING

Try bargaining in the craft markets

Malaysia is a shopper's paradise. Bargains range from duty-free electronic goods to beautiful village hand-crafts. Local batik and pewterware are world famous. Add to this a huge range of locally manufactured sportswear, leather goods and fashions. Prices are fixed in air-conditioned department stores, or *kompleks*. Elsewhere bargain for the item you fancy. Most shops accept major credit cards such as Visa, Mastercard and American Express.

Batik evolved in the 1900s when the stamp-block method was used for printing cotton textiles. The word *batik* literally means drawing with wax. Dye is applied around the free-flowing patterns and the wax is boiled off. You can watch the process in factories in Kelantan, the home of batik, and in Penang. Sarongs, shirts, skirts and batik-scarves are sold all over Malaysia.

Songket-weaving is another cottage industry on the east coast. Once the exclusive preserve of Malaysian royalty, the richly-woven cloth of gold and silver threads on silk is done by women at home. Kota Bharu is the best place to buy songket.

Selangor pewterware is one of the best buys in Malaysia. There are many retail outlets, but the best shopping spot is direct from Selangor Pewter Factory (see **Selangor**, page 66). The showroom has a range of more than 800 items, and prices are less than half what you would pay overseas.

Black ceramic-ware from Johor and Perak has a certain rustic appeal. Travellers to Sarawak have the opportunity to purchase beautiful painted pottery made in Kuching. Silverware is another cottage industry on the east coast of Peninsular Malaysia. You can buy filigree-work jewellery, where fine wire is twisted into delicate tracery, or repoussé where patterns are hammered into sheets of silver. Collectors of traditional memorabilia will be interested in the Malay *kris*, a curved silver dagger. Wood-carving is an ancient craft in Malaysia, the best artisans being commissioned by royalty. Some of the finest work is seen on traditional houses. Objects made from woven bamboo are cheap, attractive and light to carry home. The Central Market in Kuala Lumpur is a good place to browse. Baskets, lampshades and birdcages are popular buys. Last, but by no means least, is the dazzling volume of low-priced locally made and imported goods from Taiwan and Korea. Keen sportsmen will have a bonanza. Keep-fit wear and sports gear are bargain priced. So, too, are electronic goods – radios, videos, cameras, calculators – and pens and watches. Music cassettes are also good value.

ACCOMMODATION

Malaysia offers a wide range of accommodation from some of the world's most sophisticated hotels to rustic guest houses and youth hostels. Hotels are not classified by stars, or grades, but you will find internationally reputed names such as Shangri-La – frequently voted the best hotel by travellers – Regent, Hyatt and Hilton. Such top hotels can compete with any in the world for comfort, quality of service and fine dining. All have sports facilities including gymnasiums and jacuzzis, and are less expensive than comparable hotels abroad. Note that some middle range hotels charge per room/night as against single or double occupancy. Kuala Lumpur, Penang, Kota Kinabalu, Kuching and Melaka have a choice of middle range hotels, but moderately priced accommodation is difficult to find. Visitors may stay at reasonably-priced government rest houses, but you may find them full of noisy local families. A number of youth hostels offer basic accommodation for next to nothing. You do not necessarily have to be a member of the YHA, but it may save a hassle. During the low season in East Malaysia (April to September), try bargaining for a room. Hotel rates and restaurant meals are generally fixed, with a five per cent government tax and 10 per cent service charge added. Self-catering accommodation for overseas tourists is very rare. (Accommodation is listed by location in the gazetteer.)

CULTURE, ENTERTAINMENT AND NIGHTLIFE

In busy centres such as Kuala Lumpur and Penang, Western-style discothèques, nightclubs, pubs and karaoke lounges dominate Malaysia's fairly low-key nightlife. (For details see Kuala Lumpur, pages 19 and 20; other details by location in the gazetteer.) There are several venues in Kuala Lumpur which feature performances of the traditional arts.

Among the many traditional dances, look out for the *kuda kepang*. Performed by nine dancers astride two-dimensional horses, historic Muslim battles are re-enacted to the accompaniment of tambourines, gongs and other percussion instruments. From East Malaysia, *sumazu* is performed by two rows of men and women dancers dressed in elaborate costumes, where hand movements are likened to a flight of birds. *Joget* is probably the most popular national dance, and is always performed at festivals, weddings and other social occasions. Of Portuguese origin, it was introduced to Malacca by 16th-century traders. Another popular dance at social functions, *tarian inang* features performers moving to a rapid tempo as they wave brightly patterned scarves. *Tarian asyik* is renowned for its glittering costumes and graceful movements. It is said the dance originated in the royal courts of Kelantan, and the theme is the loss of the Queen's beautiful pet bird. Accompanied by gongs and drums, *tarian saba* from the Terengganu district is based on aggressive and defensive movements made by pairs of men carrying swords, shields and bells.

Another popular form of cultural entertainment is *bangsawan*, or Malay-style opera, which is said to have been introduced into Penang in the late 1800s by an Indian opera troupe. It features detailed sets and the story

Traditional Malay entertainment

Pineapples and pungent durian

always glorifies the pomp and grandeur of the old sultanates. A jerky mixture of dance, music and comedy which may not be well understood by tourists, *boria* is of Persian origin and first appeared in Penang during the late 19th century. *Jikey* is a form of traditional theatre still popular in the northwest states of Peninsular Malaysia. Folksy stories are told to a musical accompaniment of drums and tambourine. All the performers are male in the production of *mek mulong*, a traditional display of dancing and singing from the Kedah theatre. *Dondang sayang* is a favourite of the folk arts repertoire and often identified with the Straits-born Chinese. Audience participation is encouraged by the four musicians who coax a traditional tempo from a violin, a gong and a pair of frame drums. *Ghazal* evokes echoes of ancient Persia using a sitar, harmonium and, more recently, guitars. Introduction, pause, recitation and voice control all play an important part in this haunting music, which is regularly performed at weddings and other celebrations.

WEATHER AND WHEN TO GO

Both Peninsular Malaysia and the eastern states of Sabah and Sarawak experience an equatorial climate – hot, very hot, and hot and wet. There is no denying that it can be fairly debilitating. The only escape is to the cool hill stations in Pahang, northeast of KL, and in the foothills around Borneo's Gunung Kinabalu. There is also no avoiding rain at some stage of your visit. The country receives an annual average of 80-100 inches (2,000-2,500mm). As a rule, November to February is the rainy season on the east coast of Peninsular Malaysia, in northeast Sabah and western Sarawak. Terrific cloudbursts are common; at other times blanket rainfall causes serious flooding. During April to May and October, the west coast is subject to regular thunderstorms. A sticky, sunny

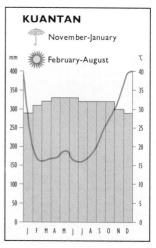

KUANTAN

November-January

February-August

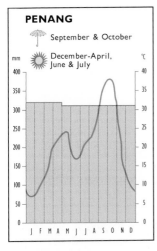

PENANG

September & October

December-April,
June & July

mm / °C

morning turns black around lunchtime and it buckets down. The extreme humidity can make Malaysia's climate very uncomfortable. A useful tip: buy a thin cotton towel in the market and wear it around your neck to mop up perspiration.

What to Wear

Casual cotton sportswear is best in Malaysia's hot climate. Women can wear shorts in Kuala Lumpur and Penang, but should dress more discreetly in the strongly Muslim state of Kelantan. Tourists of either sex should dress discreetly when visiting a mosque or temple. Topless sunbathing is rigorously forbidden. At night take a jacket or wrap for dining out in chilly air-conditioned restaurants. You do not need to dress up in the evening, though guests are always well dressed in Kuala Lumpur's top hotels. Beach resorts are more relaxed. Men

do not need a tie. You will need a sweater or jacket if you take a trip into the hills, where temperatures can be a good 10°C (50°F) below those of the lowlands.

A clear shower-cap will keep your head dry in a sudden downpour, but a plastic mac makes you sweat in the heat. If your clothes get wet, a new T-shirt costs less than a packet of cigarettes. Major hotels offer same-day laundry services at economical prices. Some towns have launderettes but they are not always easy to find. Chinese laundries and dry-cleaners, on the other hand, are not in short supply.

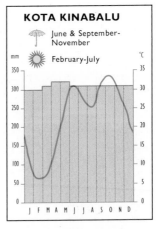

KOTA KINABALU

June & September-November

February-July

mm / °C

Give footwear some thought. Thongs, or flip-flops are lethal on slippery roads. Canvas boots are good, but hot. Easily removed casual shoes, or sandals, are ideal. Trekkers need boots with grips for scaling Gunung Kinabalu (see page 75).

HOW TO BE A LOCAL

Some knowledge of Islam, the religion of most Malays, will help to avoid the majority of social and cultural gaffes. Muslims follow the Koran for guidelines to everyday living, and the Koran requires that the faithful pray five times a day. You may be awakened by the early morning prayer-call if your hotel is near a mosque. The most important prayers are on Friday, at midday, when mosques are closed to non-Muslims. Visitors are welcome at other times. Cover your arms and legs – shorts for men, as well as women, are strictly taboo. Women may be provided with a gown. Take off your shoes at the entrance (you must do likewise for Buddhist and Hindu temples in Penang and elsewhere). Behave in a mosque as you would in a church. On no account display any intimacy towards your companion. Speak quietly if you are with a group and do not photograph people performing their ablutions, or

A traditional stilt house

A Kelantan fisherman

when they are praying. Like Muslims the world over, Malays observe the month of Ramadan. It is thoughtful, therefore, if you remember they are abstaining from eating, drinking and smoking between dawn and dusk. You may eat, but do not make a big deal of it in front of believers. You can join in the post-fast festivities in the evening, when street stalls sell special Ramadan dishes. Some Islamic states such as Kelantan observe Ramadan more strictly than others like Pulau Pinang, with its large Chinese community, or Sabah, which counts many Christians. Other aspects of mixing in local society without causing offence are merely courtesies. In a rural village, or *kampung*, do not treat local people as photo-objects. If you spot an interesting scene, ask permission before you snap away with your camera. Malays will almost always agree. Children in villages frequented by tourists may ask for money, but Malaysia is largely pressure free. A smile stretches miles when you don't speak the language but an ability to speak a few words of *Bahasa Malaysia* will win new friends. (See **Language**, page 126.)

Meeting the Iban

Malays are generally warm and laid-back, but some tribes in Sarawak have their own customs which you are advised to respect. Remember that not so long ago the Iban were head-hunters! If in doubt, consult your guide. The following are fundamental courtesies you should observe when visiting a longhouse community:

- when introduced to the chief, bow and say 'Our tuai rumah?' – how do you do?
- use both your hands when accepting beverages and food
- do not push away food which is offered you. Touch it and instead brush your lips and say thank you *(terisma kasih)*
- a white flag outside a

longhouse indicates a death. Do not enter
• do not display any Western forms of affection in front of the Ibans
• you are more than likely to be asked to pay for taking photographs, when you should demur. Some tribes in southeast Sabah may take a fancy to your clothes.

Pastimes

Most locals will be delighted to show you around, or explain the rules of a traditional pastime. The east coast is where you are more likely to come upon such activities. Your best chance is at the end of the harvest when farmers have more time.
A common local pastime in Peninsular Malaysia is top-spinning. It is a favourite game on the east coast after the harvest, with tops of various sizes – big ones in the state of Terengganu can weigh up to 11 pounds (5kg). Long-spinning contests are held, when a well balanced top may spin for two hours. Look out for advanced top-spinning contests in Kota Bharu on Wednesday and Saturday afternoons. Kite-flying is another favourite pastime said to date back to the sultan's court in 16th-century Malacca. It is also taken very seriously on the east coast. Kites are highly decorated masterpieces of bamboo and stretched paper, and they make great souvenirs. Underlining the importance of kite-flying in local life is the *wau bulan* kite logo adopted by the national air carrier MAS.
Sepak takraw, or *raga*, is a fast ball game, also said to have

been played by the royal courtiers in Malacca in the 1500s, and it is very exciting to watch. A team of six to 10 players stands in a circle about 20 feet (6m) across. The aim is to keep a rattan ball aloft as long as possible as it is kicked from player to player.
Other local games merge into art-forms. *Silat* is a self-defence discipline always performed to the rhythms of gongs and drums. You may come upon a performance at a rural celebration or wedding. The popularity of *silat* has seen it spread overseas as far away as America, but other local customs remain locked in Malay culture. *Rebana ubi* or drumming competitions are held at the end of the harvest. Judges award marks for timing, beat and style. *Wayang kulit*, a shadow-play or puppet-show, is a common evening entertainment in east coast *kampungs*. Drawn from Hindu epics such as *Ramayana*, themes reflect the cross-pollination of local cultures. A skilled *tok dalang*, the Master of Ceremonies, can operate as many as 30 puppets in a performance. There is no guarantee that you will witness a performance of these pastimes so colourfully portrayed in tourist brochures. Many such activities are spontaneous and there will be little or no advance warning. *Congkak*, a traditional board game which keeps villagers absorbed for hours has not been seen by many Malays. (Details of local cultural displays are listed by location in the gazetteer.)

CHILDREN

Malaysia is a wonderful place to take children on holiday. All hotels welcome families, even babies, and there are special rates for under-12s sharing with their parents. Menus feature half-portion meals and you will find cornflakes, rice bubbles and other familiar items on the breakfast buffet. First-class hotels have a special children's swimming-pool, games room and baby-sitting facilities. Malaysia itself is a fantasyland for the young at heart offering a choice of wonderful children's playgrounds, parks and lakes where you can hire pedal-boats, and other attractions such as butterfly farms, flower gardens and bird-parks. The orang-utan sanctuary, near Sandakan in Sabah, is of special interest to older children. Turtle-spotting near Kuala Terengganu, on the east coast, is another favourite. Traditional Malay pastimes such as top-spinning and kite-flying will keep the young and not so young enthralled. Penang in particular holds special family appeal with its sandy beaches, fascinating temples and cable-car railway. Bazaars and department stores offer outstanding buys in children's clothes, shoes and a huge variety of electronic toys.

Don'ts include the obvious, such as: don't overdo it in the heat, and don't let your child eat ice-cream or iced drinks sold in the street. Insist that a hat, T-shirt and high protection sunscreen are worn on the beach. The equatorial sun burns fair skin within minutes of exposure. Children's items, such as nappies, and Western brand-name products, are sold in department stores in Kuala Lumpur, Penang and Kota Kinabalu.

Smiles at the fish market in Kota Kinabalu

TIGHT BUDGET

At current exchange rates, Malaysia is one of the world's best holiday bargains. Travellers planning an extensive tour can cut costs by buying a special **Visit Malaysia Railpass**. You can also obtain special domestic flight coupons for the MAS **Visit Malaysia** scheme. (See details below.) Staying in middle range hotels and eating in hawker market places will keep expenses down. Check-out the food bars in large department stores like The Mall in Kuala Lumpur. Usually situated in the basement, these food bars stay open until late and sell a range of excellent foods. A family of four can eat well here for less than a quarter of the cost at home. Stock up on beer and soft drinks in a supermarket, too. Everything is much cheaper than items from a mini-bar or ordered from room service. You could fly to Malaysia with an empty suitcase and buy everything you need. Toothpaste, cosmetics and clothes are half the price you would pay in Europe, while duty-free drink and cigarettes are a third less to buy on arrival at Kuala Lumpur International Airport.
Feeling homesick? Don't phone from your room. Most hotels add a 20-30 per cent levy on overseas calls. Ask the concierge directions to the local ITT office. Take your washing with you. A Chinese laundry does it for less than half the hotel cleaning service. If it is near your hotel, the same laundry is probably doing it anyway.

Visit Malaysia Railpasses are special rail concessions for foreign travellers, valid for 30 days of unlimited travel on any class.

Visit Malaysia Airpasses, offered by MAS (the national airline), are special five-coupon air tickets valid within Peninsular Malaysia, or Sabah-Sarawak (but not inter-connecting between West and East Malaysia or between Sabah and Sarawak). The ticket is valid for a maximum of 21 days. Airpasses are sold by all MAS offices overseas. You can also purchase them in Kuala Lumpur during the first 14 days after your arrival.

SPECIAL EVENTS

Malaysia celebrates a number of colourful festivals whose dates vary according to the lunar calendar. Check with the TDC office or the concierge of your hotel.

Chinese New Year

This is celebrated some time between 21 January and 20 February. Balconies are decorated, cards are exchanged and unmarried family members and friends are given *ang pows* (small red envelopes containing money). Kuala Lumpur and Penang are especially festive. There are processions and dramatic lion

Rich batik drying in the sun

dances. Huge fire-crackers are let off to frighten away evil spirits. After 15 days, celebrations culminate in *Chap Goh Mei*. This is worth catching in Penang where it is celebrated with great gusto by local Hokkiens. Kuching, in Sarawak, celebrates *Chap Goh Mei* with a colourful Lantern Festival.

Thaipusam

Hindu devotees pay homage to Lord Muruga, youngest son of Lord Shiva. In Kuala Lumpur, there is a procession of penitents to the Batu Cave in an atmosphere electric with drumming and chanting. Skewers piercing their cheeks and nipples, they file by, apparently in a trance. Other Hindu temples may have fire-walking ceremonies.

Hari Raya Puasa

This is the Muslim festival at the end of Ramadan, the month of fasting. Although marked by a two-day national holiday, it is in essence a personal rather than a public celebration. If you are spotted in a village, someone is sure to ask you to join the feasting.

Wesak Day

This, the most important festival for Malaysian Buddhists, marks three momentous events in Buddha's life – his birthday, his enlightenment and his achievement of Nirvana. Penang and Malacca are good places to see the one-day celebrations, which take place around May.

Gawai Dyak

This is a major festival celebrated by the Dyaks,

usually in May to June, to appease the spirits. There is singing, dancing and considerable drinking of *tuak* or rice wine in the local longhouses.

Tamu Besar Harvest Festival

Feasts, cultural programmes, buffalo races and other traditional games are held in Sabah on *Tamu Besar* following the annual harvest.

Hari Raya Haji

This Muslim religious festival follows the Haj – the pilgrimage to Mecca. Prayers are offered in the mosques. An animal is sacrificed and its meat distributed among relatives and the needy.

Moon Cake Festival

Falling on the 15th day of the eighth month of the Chinese lunar calendar, the festival marks the overthrow of Mongol rulers in ancient China.

Deepvali

The Hindu 'Festival of Lights' falls during October–November. It marks the return of Rama after 14 years' exile. At some temples there are fire-walking ceremonies. *Deepvali* is a national holiday except in Sabah and Sarawak.

Christmas

Christmas is widely celebrated by Christians and non-Christians alike. Hotels and shopping complexes are decorated more brilliantly than in most cities in the West.

SPORT

Malaysia offers a huge variety of traditional and Western sports.

Climbing and Walking

Rock climbers will be able to practise on the limestone outcrops in Peninsular Malaysia. In Sabah, the ascent of Gunung Kinabalu is a two-day trek (see pages 74-5).

Malaysia's parks such as Taman Negara in Peninsular Malaysia, Kinabalu National Park in Sabah, and Niah Park in Sarawak, offer wonderful walks with opportunities for bird and butterfly watching. From Kuala Tahan in Taman Negara, you can sample many outdoor activities including nature walks, fishing and canoeing. Small groups are escorted through the jungle trails by a local guide.

Cycling

You can rent a bike for exploring Kuala Lumpur before the rush-hour begins. Longer cycling tours using an 18-gear mountain bike can be made to Selangor which is flat cycling country. For longer distance excursions, cyclists should be fit enough to travel a minimum 45 miles (70km) a day, and can overnight at rest houses.

Golf

Malaysia's premier golf club is the **Royal Selangor** in Kuala Lumpur, setting for the prestigious Malaysian Open. Near Kuala Lumpur International Airport, **Saujana Golf and Country Club** is listed among the top 100 golf courses in the world. Golfers who like a challenging course should test their skills at the **Ayer Keroh Golf and Country Club** in Melaka. At 14,000 feet (4,300m) the nine-hole **Royal Fraser's Hill**

Golf Club is short, but tricky. The par-72 **Bukit Jambul Country Club** is the crowning glory for golfers in Penang. *Golfing in Malaysia*, published by TDCM, gives a full list of golf clubs.

Scuba-diving and Snorkelling

The warm, clear waters off Peninsular Malaysia, Sabah and Sarawak are acknowledged to be some of the best diving spots in the world. A few metres below the surface are beautiful coral reefs with rainbow coloured fish, anemones and tropical shells. Turtles are also seen. In many areas, an ability to snorkel is sufficient. Other islands offer a chance of scuba-diving. Pulau Sipadan (see page 78) offers a wall dive of 2,000 feet (600m) a short distance from the beach. Redang, off the east coast state of Terengganu, is highly regarded by experienced divers. Further south, Pulau Tenggol has spectacular underwater cliffs. Served by

Saujana is a world-class course

direct flights from Kuala Lumpur, Pulau Tioman has a growing reputation among keen divers who seek more sophisticated accommodation. A number of tour operators organise inclusive island diving holidays within the five marine parks. Further information on package tours, accommodation and what to see is listed in the free brochure *Underwater Havens* published by TDCM. Most dive operators will insist on the following conditions for divers:

● proof of diver training from PADI or recognised agency
● log books or proof of advanced dives such as Deep Dives, Cave Dives and Night Dives. Without proof, you will be required to take the appropriate courses before diving
● divers who have not been diving for the past 12 months will be required to pass a refresher course

• divers are required to sign liability/waiver before or on arrival. Check your insurance cover includes acceptance of responsibility for diving accidents.

Visitors should bring their personal diving gear. Additional equipment can be rented at most centres. You should bring a torch for land use and underwater use.

White-water Rafting, Canoeing and Watersports

Other watersports such as white-water rafting and canoeing are practised in Taman Negara National Park in Pahang, Peninsular Malaysia and in Sarawak and Sabah. East Malaysia is the best centre for river sports (see pages 76 and 88).

Rafting is a year-round activity, but the best months are August to January. Most starting points are reached by four-wheel drive, although the Padas rapids (Sabah) are accessible by train. Other popular watersports such as sailing, windsurfing and waterskiing are offered by the large beach hotels lining Batu Ferringhi beach in Penang. A top watersports centre is the luxurious Pelangi Beach Resort on Langkawi – catamaran sailing, windsurfing, yachting, snorkelling and scuba-diving are all available. The Tanjung Aru beach hotel in Kota Kinabalu (Sabah) also has watersports facilities; and the Pulau Tioman resort hotels also specialise in watersports.

White-water might be a strange description of the muddy Padas but it's a white-knuckle ride

DIRECTORY

Contents

Arriving

By Air

Getting to Malaysia is easy by air. Kuala Lumpur is served by more than 20 international airlines.

British Airways operates a tri-weekly Boeing 747 service from the UK's Heathrow terminal 4. The Monday–Friday service transits through Madras and the Thursday service via Bangkok. Both cities are optional stop-overs. ITN news is a feature of all BA long-haul services.

Sydney is linked to Kuala Lumpur via Singapore on a four-times-weekly flight from Australia. The airline also has a weekly direct flight Kuala Lumpur–Auckland. Many Antipodeans travel on the BA 009 and stop off for a holiday in Malaysia.

(There is a British Airways APEX fare to Kuala Lumpur available – no advance purchases, minimum stay seven days.)

Passengers can also travel overland to Singapore and return on the BA Changi–Heathrow service.

BA Offices Abroad

British Airways Reservations in Kuala Lumpur: Mezzanine Floor, See Hoy Chan Plaza, Jalan Raja Chulan (tel: 2325797).

BA Reservations in Sydney: Level 26, Maritime Centre 26th level, 201-207 Kent Street 2000 (tel: (02) 258 3244).

BA Reservations in Auckland: Dilworth Building, corner Queen/Custom Street (tel: (09) 33049).

BA Reservations in New York: 530 5th Avenue, NY 10036 (tel: (718) 397 4580).

The national flag-carrier MAS (Malaysia Airlines System) is handling agent for all overseas airlines in Malaysia including BA. The airline operates direct flights to Malaysia from Europe and the Middle East, and with Qantas from six points in Australia.

Flying time from London–Kuala

Lumpur is about 14 hours, from the US 18–20 hours, from Australia four–nine hours.

MAS Reservations in London: 191 Askew Road W12 9AX (tel: 081-862 0770).

Kuala Lumpur International Airport is located at Subang, 15 miles (24km) from town (about 45 minutes' drive to the city centre). It is a huge modern airport with excellent duty-free shops, bank, postal and international telecommunications, restaurants and bars. Free trolley and porter service.

International and domestic departure tax is payable.

By Rail

Many visitors to Malaysia arrive by rail. The railway network extends from Singapore, through the main towns and up to Thailand on both the east and west coast.

By Road

An extensive road network throughout West Malaysia links most of the major towns of tourist interest – from Singapore in the south, to Thailand in the north. (See **Driving**.)

Getting to Kuala Lumpur

For visitors arriving at Subang International Airport, there is a frequent bus service to the centre of Kuala Lumpur. Or you can take a taxi – they work on a voucher system. Go to the voucher desk. Some hotels have courtesy buses.

Kuala Lumpur can be reached by rail either from Singapore or travelling south from Butterworth (in Pulau Pinang). Taxis are available from the station to any part of town.

The capital is accessible by shared **out-station taxi** from most major towns in Peninsular Malaysia.

You can also reach Kuala Lumpur by **Express Bus** from Singapore, Butterworth and Kota Bharu. The main bus terminal is Pudu Raya Terminal in Jalan Pudu. There is a comfortable hotel on the fourth floor if you arrive tired.

Entry Formalities

All visitors require a passport valid for at least six months beyond the intended stay in Malaysia. An onward or return ticket and proof of sufficient funds for the proposed stay are also necessary. Anyone considered scruffy or unsuitably dressed may be refused entry. British and Commonwealth citizens and US nationals do not require a visa to enter Malaysia. The visa-free concession is valid for three months. Social visitors can extend this stay to six months without pre-conditions. You must complete a

At Penang Butterfly Farm

disembarkation form on arrival. Airport immigration officers will return the embarkation portion. Keep this safe for presentation on departure.

Camping

There are a few official camping grounds in Malaysia, but there is now a law to prevent you from erecting a tent wherever takes your fancy. Nice sites exist along the undeveloped east coast and on offshore islands. Lake Chini, 60 miles (100km) from Kuantan, has rustic chalets and camping

spots. Trekkers and fishermen can camp beside Kenyir Dam. There are no facilities, so bring everything for survival. Mosquito repellent and coils are essential.

Chemist (see **Pharmacies**)

Crime

Malaysia is relatively safe for tourists, but take the precaution of leaving your valuables in the hotel safe. Carry only what you need in a safe place on your person. Kota Kinabalu in Sabah

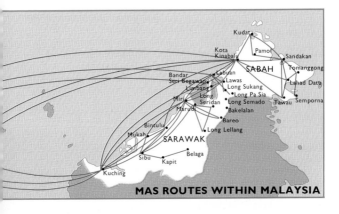

MAS ROUTES WITHIN MALAYSIA

DIRECTORY

Low-tide at Marang

has experienced problems with bag-snatchers, so take extra care there. If you need help, or lose an item of value, contact the Tourist Police: obtain a copy of your statement for insurance records. Crimes of violence against tourists are unknown. Note that dropping litter is a serious offence – a cigarette carelessly dropped can carry a M$50 fine. See also **Drugs, Police**.

Customs Regulations

Malaysian customs allow the import of 200 cigarettes, a litre of spirits, and perfume not exceeding M$200 in value. Purchases can be made at Kuala Lumpur International Airport. Duty-free items sell for considerably less than at British airports. Customs officials usually require you to open one suitcase. Tourists are warned that the import of drugs into Malaysia carries the death penalty.

Disabled People

Malaysia is not recommended for disabled travellers, because of the heat and the difficulty in getting about. Note that most temples have only stairway access.

There is a representative of **Rehabilitation International** in Kuala Lumpur who may be able to supply details of wheelchair hire, etc. Write to: YDH Dato EJ Lawrence, Lot 339, 3rd Floor, Wisma MPI, Jalan Raja Chulan. The following hotels have facilities for the disabled:

Penang Mutiara Beach Resort, Penang. For reservations contact Leading Hotels of the World, UK tel: (0800) 181123; US tel: (800) 223 6800.

Park Royal, Kuala Lumpur. For reservations contact THF Worldwide Reservations, UK tel: (0345) 500400; US tel: (913) 831 3535.

Holiday Inns have a number of hotels in Malaysia with facilities for the disabled; for more details, telephone (071) 722 7755 (UK) or (312) 932 5800 (US).

Driving

Peninsular Malaysia is an attractive proposition for self-drive. Some companies offer self-drive packages including accommodation. More than 11,000 miles (18,000km) of tarred roads link Johor Bahru to the Thai border and the Straits of Malacca to the South China Sea. Most are in very good condition.

There are toll charges on some highways. The East-West Highway between Butterworth and Kota Bharu is excellent. Double carriageways are under construction on congested sections between Kuala Lumpur, Alor Setar and Johor Bahru. Trucks on these sections make driving unpleasant.

The only deterrent to a self-drive holiday is posed by local drivers who flout traffic rules. On country roads you may be the only motorist.

Visiting drivers require a valid International Driving Licence. Seatbelts are compulsory for the driver and front-seat passenger. Driving is on the left, and the speed limit on expressways and highways is 68mph (110kph), 50mph (80kph) on trunk roads, and 31mph (50kph) in urban areas. Cars are air-conditioned. There are frequent petrol stations with WC facilities and drinks; credit cards are accepted. A drop-off fee is usually applicable between Kuala Lumpur and Johor Bahru/ Penang and vice versa.

There is a Malaysian Automobile Association – head office at 25 Jalan Yap Kwan Seng, Kuala Lumpur (tel: 2425777). There are offices in most states.

Parking is very difficult in Kuala Lumpur and other large towns. There are relatively few parking meters and an abundance of parking meter wardens who make no allowances for visitors.

Car Rental Companies

Avis Rent A Car: 40 Jalan Sultan Ismail, Kuala Lumpur (tel: 2423500).

Budget Rent a Car: 20A Jalan Telawi Bangsar Baru, Kuala Lumpur (tel: 2551044).

Hertz Rent a Car: Lot 214A Kompleks Antarabangsa, Jalan Sultan Ismail, Kuala Lumpur (tel: 2421014).

Words on Road Signs

UTARA   North
SELATAN   South
TIMUR   East
BARAT   West
AWAS   Caution
IKUT KIRI   Keep left
KURANGKAN LAJU   Slow down
JALAN SEHALA   One way
LENCONGAN   Detour
BERHENTI   Stop
BERI LALUAN   Give way
HAD LAJU   Speed limit
DILARANG MEMOTONG   No overtaking

Drugs

Malaysia has one of the strictest drug policies in the world. The message is simple: get caught in possession of an illegal substance and you will hang. Pictures of the hangman's noose are displayed at all points of entry. The trip to the scaffold is not quick: offenders are likely to languish several years in jail. **Do not take the risk**.

Electricity

The main voltage in Malaysia is 220 volts AC. If you bring electrical equipment with 110 volts, pack a converter. Up-market hotels will supply one.

DIRECTORY

Embassies and Consulates

Australian High Commission: 6 Jalan Yap Kwan Seng, KL (tel: 2423122).

Canadian High Commission: 7th Floor, Plaza MBF, Jalan Ampang, KL (tel: 2612000).

New Zealand High Commission: 193 Jalan Tun Razak, KL (tel: 2486422).

UK High Commission: 185 Jalan Ampang, KL (tel: 2482122).

US Embassy: 376 Jalan Tun Razak, KL (tel: 2489011).

Emergency Telephone Number

Fire, police and ambulance: 999

Entertainment Information

Malaysia does not yet have a 'What's On' guide to entertainment. Ask your hotel concierge or check the local newspapers (see **Media**). The local TDCM (Tourist Development Corporation) office should be able to provide information on cultural events.

Entry Formalities (see Arriving)

Health

Immunisation against typhoid, hepatitis A, polio and tetanus is recommended for visitors to Malaysia. Anti-malarial precautions are also advised, but no vaccinations are compulsory unless coming from a yellow-fever zone. Dengue fever is increasing in poor urban areas.

Stomach upsets are usually caused by eating hot, spicy food rather than contaminated products. Anti-diarrhoeal tablets should clear the problem in 24 hours. Treatment with water and re-hydration salts is recommended. If the trouble does not clear up, ask your hotel to locate a doctor. First-class hotels supply boiled water for guests. Elsewhere use water purification tablets or drink bottled mineral water. Use sunscreen protection cream (factor +15) outdoors and do not remain exposed to the sun for more than one hour at a time. People who sweat profusely may need to take a salt supplement. Beware of catching a tropical cold in air-conditioned hotels. See also **Pharmacies**.

Holidays

1 January **New Year's Day**, January/February **Chinese New Year**, March/April **Hari Raya Puasa**, 1 May **Labour Day**, 27 May **Wesak Day**, 5 June **Birthday of His Majesty the Yang di-Pertuan Agong**, July/August **Hari Raya Haji**, 31 August **'National Day'**, October/November **Deepvali**, 17 December **Birthday of the Prophet Muhammad**, 25 December **Christmas Day**.

State Holidays

Various events are celebrated as holidays in the individual states. These include the birthdays of the state rulers and festivals of particular ethnic groups, such as Thaipusam at the end of January (Negeri Sembilan, Perak, Pulau Pinang and Selangor only) and Gawai Dyak in June (Sarawak only).

Lost Property

In truth, there is little hope of recovering lost property. Ensure you have adequate insurance cover before leaving on holiday. To make a claim, obtain a written report of your loss from either your hotel, or the police.

Media

Newspapers

Major Western newspapers such as the *International Herald Tribune, Daily Telegraph, European*, etc, arrive one to two days late in hotel bookshops in Kuala Lumpur, Penang, Sabah and Sarawak. The main English language broadsheet, the *New Straits Times*, is published daily and sold throughout Peninsular and East Malaysia. Sabah also publishes the *Borneo Mail, Daily Express* and *Sabah Times*. Top hotels deliver local papers free to guests.

Radio

BBC World Service broadcasts to Malaysia on: 6.195 khz or 48.43 metres (05.00–08.30 hrs); 3.915 khz or 76.63 metres (06.00–07.15 hrs and 11.00–12.15 hrs); 9.740 khz or 30.80 metres (05.00–12.15 hrs).

Television

There is an English language television news broadcast at 19.00 hrs; ONN TV News is received by major tourist hotels.

Money Matters

The unit of currency in Malaysia is the *ringgit* or Malaysian dollar (M$) which divides into 100 *sen*. Notes are issued in denominations of M$1, M$10, M$20, M$50, M$100, M$500 and M$1,000. Coins come in denominations of M$1 and 50, 20, 10, 5 and 1 *sen*. Visitors may import M$10,000. No limit is imposed on other currencies or

travellers' cheques. Banks are open for travellers on flights at international airports. The best rates are available at the airport and from local money changers. Exchange rates are published daily in newspapers and on TV news bulletins. Few hotels offer the current rate; shop around for the best deal. Credit cards are widely accepted. Banks charge commission on travellers' cheque conversions.

Opening Times

Shops

Generally shops are open from 09.30–19.00 hrs, while supermarkets and departmental stores operate from 10.00–22.00 hrs. In Johor, Kedah, Perlis, Kelantan and Terengganu, the public holiday is Friday instead of Sunday, so some shops may be closed.

Government Offices

Government office hours are as follows:
Monday–Thursday: 08.00 to 12.45 hrs, 14.00 to 16.15 hrs.
Friday: 08.00 to 12.15 hrs, 14.45 to 16.15 hrs.
Saturday: 08.00–12.45 hrs.
In Johor, Kedah, Perlis, Kelantan and Terengganu, government offices are open from 08.00 to 12.45 hrs on Thursdays and are closed on Fridays.

Banks

Monday–Friday: 10.00–15.00 hrs.
Saturday: 09.30–11.30 hrs.
In Kedah, Perlis, Kelantan and Terengganu, banks are open 09.30–11.30 hrs Thursday and closed on Friday.
Museums: see individual entries.

DIRECTORY

Thai temple, Penang

Personal Safety

Crimes of violence are common in Malaysia, but they do not usually involve tourists. Provided you observe certain rules, your visit should be trouble free. Do not carry passport, airline ticket or more cash than you need. Be especially vigilant in street markets. Do not take short cuts down deserted streets at night in Kuala Lumpur. Be a little more careful in Kota Kinabalu and Sandakan where there are populations of poor refugees. Young foreign women may provoke sexual comment from Malay youths, but tourists in general are free from harassment. There are more beggars on the streets of London than there are in all Malaysia.

For your own personal safety it is advised to bathe only on patrolled hotel beaches.

Pharmacies

There are many pharmacies and Chinese herbal remedy shops in Malaysia. Most are adequately stocked for minor ailments – stomach upsets, flu, etc.

Large department stores such as **Yaohan** sell pharmaceutical and personal requirements. In all cases take what you are likely to need, especially if visiting remote parts of Sabah and Sarawak.

In Kuala Lumpur are:
Allied Pharmacy: 53 Jalan Sultan; **Kuala Lumpur Pharmacy:** 78 Jalan Bintang; **Pacific Pharmacy:** Lot 059 Sungei Wang Plaza. Also **Guardian Pharmacy**, a large chain which has a branch in virtually every shopping complex.

Chinese medical shops are found in the Central Market in Kuala Lumpur. Hotel drug-stores usually sell a small range of pain-killers, cough lozenges, toothpaste, etc.

Places of Worship

While predominantly Muslim, Malaysia allows freedom of worship to many other religions. As well as mosques, there are Chinese, Buddhist and Hindu temples and Christian churches. There are no synagogues. Ask your hotel concierge to check the times of services in the following churches in Kuala Lumpur (Christian churches are also found in Penang, Melaka, Johor, Kota Kinabalu and Kuching).

Evangelical Lutheran Church: 21 Jalan Abdul Samad.
Baptist Church: 70 Jalan Hicks.
Seventh Day Adventist Mission: 2-B Jalan Walter Grenier.
Saint Andrew's Presbyterian Church: 31 Jalan Weld.

Saint Francis Xavier Jesuit Church: Jalan Gasing, Petaling Jaya.
Saint John's Roman Catholic Cathedral: Bukit Nanas.
Saint Mary's Anglican Church: Jalan Raja.
Wesley Methodist Church: Jalan Wesley.

Police

Malaysian policemen are generally friendly and helpful to tourists. Whether you have any success in reporting a crime is another matter. The area where they are inordinately efficient is in arresting suspected drug-traffickers. Be warned!
Tourist police are identified by the chequered band on their caps. All speak English.

Police Station Locations:
Johor: Balai Polis Central Johor, Johor Bahru (tel: (07) 245222).
Kedah: Balai Polis Central Kedah, Jalan Stadium, Alor Setar (tel: (04) 735222).
Kelantan: Balai Polis Central Kelantan, Kota Bharu (tel: (09) 785522).
Kuala Lumpur: Balai Polis Central Malaysia, Jalan Hang Tuah (tel: (03) 2415522).
Malacca: Balai Polis Central Melaka, Jalan Kota, Melaka (tel: (06) 222222).
Negeri Sembilan: Balai Polis Central Negeri Sembilan, Seremban (tel: (06) 722222).
Pahang: Balai Polis Central Pahang, Jalan Gambut, Kuantan (tel: (09) 522222).
Perak: Balai Polis Central Perak, Ipoh (tel: (05) 535522).
Perlis: Balai Polis Central Perlis, Kangar (tel: (04) 762222).
Sabah: Balai Polis Central Sabah, Kota Kinabalu (tel: (088) 212222).

Sarawak: Balai Polis Central Sarawak, Jalan Bandaruddin, Kuching (tel: (082) 245522).

Post Office

The Malaysian postal service is not the fastest in the world. Count on 8–14 days for an air-mail item to reach Europe from Kuala Lumpur. Most tourist hotels supply stamps. If using the central post office, post your letter in the box marked *Lain-Lain Tempat* ('other places/foreign mail'). KL's post office is:
Pejabat Pos Besar Kuala Lumpur: 2nd Floor, Dayabumi Complex (tel: 2741122).

Public Transport

Malaysia has a cheap, efficient public transport system. You can travel anywhere in the country using air, rail, road and local ferry services. Taxi is the best way to commute within a town – the flagfall in Kuala Lumpur costs less than a box of matches in Britain.

Air

MAS (Malaysian Airlines System) domestic service links

Advertising a fortune teller

the federal capital with Ipoh, Penang, Alor Setar, Langkawi, Kota Bharu, Kuala Terengganu, Kuantan, Johor Bahru, Kota Kinabalu, Lahad Datu, Labuan, Kuching, Bintulu, Sandakan, Sibu and Miri. On a number of these sectors, the airline provides special economy tourist flights at night. Domestic airports provide basic facilities – those in popular destinations such as Penang and Sandakan are excellent. Meals are served on the Peninsular Malaysia–East Malaysia sectors. Cabin crews speak English and are kind and attentive. Check in one hour prior to departure. MAS and Singapore Airlines operate a joint shuttle service between Kuala Lumpur and Singapore. Tickets may be purchased at special counters in both Subang (KL) and Changi (Singapore) airports. Seating is on a first-come-first-served basis.

MAS Reservations are available from:

33rd Floor, Bangunan MAS, Jalan Sultan Ismail, KL (tel: 2610555);

Ground Floor, Menara Utama UMBC, Jalan Sultan Sulaiman, KL (tel: 2305115);

Lot 157 First Floor Complex Dayabumi, Jalan Sultan Sulaiman, KL (tel: 2748734);

Lot 7A 3rd Floor, Pan Pacific Hotel, Jalan Putra, KL (tel: 4426759);

4th Floor, Tun Abdul Razak Complex, Penang Road, Penang (tel: 620011);

10th Floor, Kompleks Karamunsing Jalan Selatan, Kota Kinabalu, Sabah (tel: 51455);

Bagunan MAS Lot 215 Song Thian Cheok Road, 93100,

Kuching, Sarawak (tel: 246622). Domestic departures/arrivals from Subang Kuala Lumpur International Airport terminal 2. There is a nominal domestic departure tax payable.

For further information call 7461014/7464646.

Rail

The Malaysian railway system (KTM Keretapi Tanah Melayu) is comfortable and economical – you can travel third class from Kuala Lumpur to Singapore for the equivalent of a McDonald's hamburger. Two main passenger lines operate. The west coast line from Singapore to Kuala Lumpur and Butterworth (for Penang) links with Thai railways on the border. A branch line from Gemas travels up the northeast coast to Kota Bharu. It also joins Thai railways. There are a number of services. Express trains stopping only at major towns are recommended to tourists. 'Visit Malaysia Railpasses', for 10 days' or 30 days' unlimited travel, are valid on any class. Sleeping berths are extra. Family groups (minimum four persons) are entitled to a 25 per cent discount, students are allowed 50 per cent.

Kuala Lumpur and Ipoh are known for their splendid mainline stations with attached colonial-style hotels.

News-stands, refreshments, exchange facilities, WC and left luggage depot are available.

Kuala Lumpur Reservations: 2477435.

Buses

Three types of long distance

Trishaws can be an expensive treat

buses operate in Malaysia. Non-air-conditioned between the various states (not recommended), non-air-conditioned within the state (not recommended) and air-conditioned express buses connecting all major towns (not recommended if you have a heart condition). Tickets are cheap; however, the bus may not depart on time.

Long-distance Taxis
These are a better bet than a hot, cramped bus. A flat rate is shared between four passengers. The driver leaves only when he has a full load. Out-station taxis are inexpensive. You can also charter a taxi for a day's sightseeing. Check the driver speaks English and agree a fare.

Trishaws
These pedal carriages are available in some places (Penang and Melaka). Agree a fare; it should not exceed M\$2 per kilometre.

Senior Citizens
Some elderly people will find the equatorial climate difficult to cope with. Sightseeing in Malaysia also involves a considerable amount of climbing. Anyone reasonably fit, staying in a comfortable hotel, should be able to accomplish short tours and shopping expeditions. Longer journeys are not recommended. SAGA Holidays include Malaysia in their programme – their holidays are specifically designed for senior citizens. For more information contact **Saga Holidays Ltd**, Saga Building, Middleburg Square, Folkestone, Kent CT20 1AZ, UK (tel: (0303) 85700); or, in the US, Saga International, 120 Boylston Street, Boston, Mass (tel: (617) 451 6808).

Student and Youth Travel
Malaysia is one of the world's most appealing places for youth travel. Not only is the cost of living cheap, it offers a huge range of activity holidays for the energetic walker, climber or diver. Sabah is highly recommended for youth holidays. Trained guides

accompany all adventure tours. Concessions are available for holders of student-cards in hostels, etc. See **Tight Budget** (page 108).

Telecommunications

Malaysia has an advanced telecommunications system. Most major hotels have IDD (international direct dialling) from your room – to obtain an outside line dial 9. Calls are more expensive when placed via a hotel operator/outside exchange. Overseas telephone calls can be made from public telephones at the Central Telegraph Office, Bukit Mahkamah in Kuala Lumpur – open 24 hours. Public telephones in Malaysia are coin or card operated – cards can be purchased from most retail outlets. International card-calls can also be made from Kuala Lumpur International Airport. To call Malaysia the country code is 60 (code for KL if dialling from abroad is 3). To call Malaysia from Australia,

dial 0011 60, then the city code without the first zero and then the number you require. Similarly from Canada dial 011 60, from Eire 16 60, from New Zealand 00 60, from UK 010 60 and from US 011 60.

To telephone out of Malaysia, dial the international access code which is 007, then the country code and then the subscriber's number (do not include the first zero in the subscriber's area code). From Malaysia to Australia dial 007 61, Canada 007 1, Eire 007 353, New Zealand 007 64, UK 007 44, US 007 1.

Useful Numbers

Directory information   103
Trunk calls and operator
   assisted calls   101
Weather report (KL)   1052

Time

Time throughout Malaysia is eight hours ahead of GMT, the same or two hours later than Australia, 11½–17 hours ahead of Canada, 13–19 hours ahead of the US and four hours later than New Zealand.

Tipping

Though not encouraged, tipping is becoming common in Malaysia. Porters in international hotels expect a tip for errands – around M$2–3 for carrying luggage. Hotels add a 10 per cent cover charge per bill. Leaving small change is appreciated by waiters. Tour guides should be tipped about 10 per cent of the cost of your tour if you are satisfied.

Toilets

Finding a WC is usually no problem in most large towns or

A hazard on the East-West highway

sites of tourist interest. *Tandas* means toilet, *Perempuan*, women and *Lelaki*, men. Most are Western style and relatively clean. Always carry toilet paper. WC and ablutions facilities are found in most petrol stations.

Tourist Offices

Local
TDC Malaysia Head Office, 24th–27th Floor, Menara Dato Onn, Putra World Trade Centre, Jalan Tun Ismail, Kuala Lumpur (tel: 2935188).
Malaysia Tourist Information Complex, Lot 109, Jalan Ampang, Kuala Lumpur (tel: 2434929).
TDC Southern Region, No 1, 4th Floor, Kompleks Tun Abdul Razak, Jalan Wong Ah Fook, Johor Bahru (tel: (07) 223591).
TDC Northern Region, 10 Jalan Tun Syed Sheikh Barakbah, 10200 Pulau Pinang (tel: (04) 620066/619067).
TDC East Coast Region, 2243 Ground Floor, Wisma MCIS, Jalan Sultan Zainal Abidin, Kuala Terengganu (tel: (09) 621893/621433).
TDC Sarawak, 2nd Floor, AIA Building, Bukit Mata Kuching, Jalan Song Thian Cheok, Kuching (tel: (082) 246575/246775).
TDC Sabah, Ground Floor, Wisma Wing Onn Life, No 1 Jalan Segunting, Kota Kinabalu (tel: (088) 211698/211732).

Overseas
UK: Tourist Development Corporation Malaysia, 57 Trafalgar Square, London WC2N 5DU (tel: 071-930 7932).
Australia: Tourist Development Corporation Malaysia, 65 York Street, Sydney, NSW (tel: (02) 294441/2).
Canada: Malaysia Tourist Information Center, 830 Burrard Street, Vancouver, BC V6Z ZK4 (tel: (604) 681-0208).
US: Malaysia Tourist Information Center, 818 West 7th Street, Los Angeles, CA 90017 (tel: (213) 689-9702).

Travel Agencies
Major travel companies have headquarters in Kuala Lumpur. Tours range from city highlights and cultural programmes to wilderness adventure holidays and activity tours.
Recommended are:
Angkasa Travel Service, Angkasa Raya Building Lot 1.14 and 1.15, First Floor, Jalan Ampang, Kuala Lumpur (tel: 2486566).
Borneo Expeditions, Unit 306, 3rd Floor, Wisma Sabah, Jalan Tun Razak, Kota Kinabalu, Sabah (tel: (088) 222721).
Gasi Travel Centre, Suite 101, 1st Floor, Bangunan Yayasan Selangor, Jalan Bukit Bintang, Kuala Lumpur (tel: 2437522).
Jet-Era Travel and Tours, 39 Jalan Raja Chulan, Kuala Lumpur (tel: 2308362).
Mayflower Acme Tours, 18 Jalan Segambut Pusat, Kuala Lumpur (tel: 6267011).
Inter-Pacific, 75 Jalan Bukit Bintang, Kuala Lumpur (tel: 2480011/2480062).
Tour East, 603 Penang Plaza, Burmah Road, Penang (tel: (04) 362315).
Vacasia Tours and Travel, 279 Jalan Perkasa Satu, Taman Maluri, Cheras, Kuala Lumpur (tel: 9844055).

LANGUAGE

Bahasa Malaysia is the official language in Malaysia but as it is a multi-racial country, you will hear many languages. English is very widely spoken. People in former British Borneo are especially fluent English-speakers and most Kuala Lumpur taxi-drivers know some words. Bahasa Malaysia is a colourful mixture of many other tongues – including Sanskrit, Arabic and English. As a general guide pronounce:

a   as in bar
ai   as in aisle
au as in the 'ow' of cow
g   rather hard, as in girl
h   sounded, as in halt
i   like a double 'e' – feet
j   like the English 'j' – jump
o   like the English 'o' in hot
u   as a long 'oo', as in tool

Pronouns
I saya
you anda, awak, encik (Mr), cik (Miss), puan (Mrs)
we kami
he/she dia
they mereka

Questions
can you help me? bolehkah encik tolong saya?
how do I get there? bagaimanakah saya boleh ke sana?
how far? berapa jauh?
how long will it take? berapa lama?
how much? (price) berapa harganya?
what is this/that? apakah ini/itu?
what is your name sir? siapa nama encik?
when? bila?
where? di mana?
why? mengapa?

Directions
go up naik
go down turun
turn belok
right kanan
left kiri
front hadapan
behind belakang
north utara
south selatan
east timur
west barat

Numbers
one satu
two dua
three tiga
four empat
five lima
six enam
seven tujuh
eight lapan
nine sembilan
ten sepuluh
eleven sebelas
twelve dua belas
twenty dua puluh
one hundred seratus

Useful words and expressions
a little sedikit
a lot banyak
beach pantai
beef daging lembu
chicken ayam
cold sejuk
crab ketam
drink minum
do not have tiada
eat makan
excuse me maafkan saya
female perempuan
fish ikan
fruit buah
have ada
hot panas
I am sorry saya minta maaf
male lelaki
meat daging

INDEX/ACKNOWLEDGEMENTS

The Automobile Association wishes
to thank the following photographers
and libraries for their assistance in
the preparation of this book.

CHRISTINE OSBORNE
photographed those pictures not
listed below:

MARY EVANS PICTURE LIBRARY 8
Bombarding Selangor, 9 Attack on
Kolah Lama

NATURE PHOTOGRAPHERS LTD 89
Rainforest, 90 Vegetation, 94 Fruit
bat (S C Bisserot)

Author's Acknowledgements
The author wishes to thank the
following people who assisted with
research: Fatima Norbinsha (TDC
London); Zahariah Kahar (Penang
Mutiara Hotel); Hoichai Teow
(Tourist Guide, Kuala Lumpur); Siew
Yong Gnanalingam (MAS, Kuala
Lumpur); Shamsiah Sanin; Elizabeth
Lam (Inter-Pacific, Sabah); Rosemary
Wee (Shangri-La Hotel Kuala
Lumpur); Shamsuddin Salleh
(Perkass Hotel, Mt Kinabalu); Sii Hou
Hoo (Borneo Expeditions, Kota
Kinabalu); and especially Razaleigh
Zianal (TDCM, Kuala Lumpur).